Supporting the Ambitions of Higher Education

Refresh. Reshape. Redesign.

Edited by Alison Poot

Published by Pebble Learning Ltd

e-Innovation Centre
University of Wolverhampton
Shifnal Road
Telford
TF2 9FT
UK

First published 2024
© Pebble Learning 2024

ISBN: 978-0-9565641-7-7

The right of Alison Poot to be identified as the editor of this work has been asserted in accordance with Section 77 and 78 of the Copyright, Designs and Patents Act 1988.

All rights reserved. No part of this publication may be reproduced, stored in a retrieval system or reproduced or transmitted in any form or by any means, electronic, mechanical, photocopying, recording or otherwise, without the prior written permission of the publishers. This book may not be lent, resold, hired out or otherwise disposed of by way of trade in any form of binding or cover other than that in which it is published, without the prior consent of the publishers.

Design & cover: Pebble Learning

Contents

	An introduction by Shane Sutherland	IX
1	Introducing PebblePad from the ground up: It's a bumpy road to the top *Peter Kilgour, Kevin Petrie, & Carole Hunter*	5
2	IReimagining eportfolios for learning and employment: A case study in Interior Design *Hailey Bassiri, Hailey Bell, Paola Gavilanez & Gillian Sudlow*	21
3	Creative portfolios and developmental trackers: Use of PebblePad in the School of Education at The University of Sheffield *Hadrian Cawthorne & Cat Bazela*	26
4	Casting the net wide: The "conflict of efficiencies" and large scale PebblePad workflows at the University of Edinburgh. *Robert Chmielewski*	33
5	Enhancing professional identity and capability in a transdisciplinary programme through ongoing reflection using PebblePad. *Buena Jill Galleposo, Susanne Lorenz, Cathy Malone, & Harriet Thew*	41
6	More than IT support: The role of the PebblePad Coordinator *Sheridan Gardiner-Klose & Dr. Jennifer Masters*	48
7	Enhancing collaboration and content sharing across multiple Higher Educational Institutes with PebblePad *Dr. Louise Grisedale*	54
8	Windows and Mirrors: a view into practice, the evolving professional capability of students and an invitation to examine our own reflection *Dr. Linda Jaffray, John Cooper, Leigh Harkness, Kathryn Terry, Dr. Yang Yang, Bob Wylie*	61
9	From Literacy Skills to Skills Literacy: Supporting students' skills articulation through PebblePad as an eportfolio tool *Becky Lees, Barry Avery & Daniel Russell*	66
10	Developing a multi-site, asynchronous assessment in a large, dispersed medicine course *Jennifer Lindley*	71
11	Student organization event planning, review, and reflection: Workbook approvals, assessment data, and student leaders as Workspace Managers *Andrew Longhofer*	76
12	Uptake and use of PebblePad Alumni Accounts by Australian graduates *Dr. Jennifer Masters*	81

13	Student-Led, Individually-Created Courses (SLICCs): A reflection-based experiential learning and assessment framework using an eportfolio, scalable to support institutional Curriculum Transformation *Dr. Gavin McCabe & Professor Simon C Riley*	89
14	Using PebblePad for authentic assessment in ways that might not have been envisaged *Paul McLaughlin*	95
15	ePortfolios go to the Parks: Lessons learned from Honors Immersive Service-Learning and Leadership Academic Programs *Dr. Chelsea Redger-Marquardt, Dr. Kimberly Engber & Aaron Valentine*	81
16	Extending the use of PebblePad to meet Australian Nursing standards and organisational vision through AAA signature pedagogy *Jo-Anne Rihs*	106
17	Transforming a student placement portfolio: A seven-year evolution towards personalised learning and success *Rebecca Scriven & Brooke Chapman*	115
18	Redefining success: PebblePad's journey to reputation recovery *Joseph Spink & David Price*	121
19	Folio Thinking: Teaching to a different test *Sonja Taylor*	125
20	Integrating PebblePad to adapt the Student-Led, Individually Created Course Model into a Master of Public Health Capstone Course: What we learned *Jennifer Yessis, Katherine Lithgow & Nada El-Abbar*	131
21	Empowering Community Care Licensing Education: Leveraging eportfolios for inclusivity, flexibility, and skill enhancement *Junsong Zhang, Albertine De Leon, & Ben Coulas*	137

Index	149

PebbleBash 2024

Refresh | Reshape | Redesign

Introduction by Shane Sutherland, CEO

It is a pleasure, a delight and, I suppose, a bit of a surprise to be writing the introduction to this book of case studies 20 years after the birth of PebblePad, and 14 years after our very first PebbleBash. In being honoured with this task I thought it would be wise to look back at our earlier PebbleBash books, six in all, to seek inspiration for this latest introduction.

Back in 2010 I wrote:

> These case studies begin to capture some of the unique affordances of the personal learning system, PebblePad. It is a tool wholly founded on improving learning and we believe it to be without equal. However, it is just a tool – albeit one which is based on sound educational principles and borne out of extensive pedagogical practice. As a tool it relies on the people who use it to use it knowingly, insightfully and deliberatively.

I think that the case studies we see mustered here 14 years later bear witness to the innovative and inspiring educators, learning designers and other professions helping to improve the learning experience and learning outcomes for all the students with whom they engage. This will undoubtedly be reflected in the presentations at the conference itself. PebblePad is a great platform, but it's always been the people who bring it to life and do remarkable things with it.

I also wrote that the use of PebblePad and the pedagogies it supported was disruptive in nature, requiring immense effort, resilience and fortitude. To some extent it's still true that an element of risk taking is required whenever innovation is present, and so the educational and developmental environments in which PebblePad is used need to be supportive of such risk taking. They weren't always so, but it's getting easier.

I argued that use at an institutional level requires insight and leadership. It requires a commitment to the oft espoused rhetoric that *the graduates of this university are more than the sum of their subject knowledge.* Much has changed since 2010, more-so across the span of 20 years, and yet one of today's most pressing questions for senior educational leaders concerns the very value of the higher education experience. It makes sense then that higher education is moving inexorably beyond content as the primary currency of learning. Curricula are increasingly enhanced with rich experiences that provide opportunities for students to develop, rehearse and improve a broad repertoire of skills, competencies and capabilities, equipping them for success, helping them become career- and future-ready. This is increasingly the norm - and of course PebblePad is designed to support exactly this kind of learning.

Despite there being much closer alignment between what we do, and how this directly supports the needs of higher education, we still find it difficult to put a label on what PebblePad actually is. It was ever thus! Looking back across our PebbleBashes we have described the platform as a *personal learning system*, as a *personal learning space* and with the aid of our audience at the 2018 'Bash as a *learning journey platform*. We have described PebblePad as *not just an ePortfolio* and as *much more than an ePortfolio*, but never just as an ePortfolio! Back in 2010 I tried to elaborate on this providing a definition of what an ePortfolio was:

> *A purposeful aggregation of digital items – ideas, evidence, reflections, feedback etc, which presents a selected audience with evidence of a person's learning and/or ability.*

…and how PebblePad was different:

> *…a personal place …where my thoughts, ideas and aspirations can be more easily articulated through the supporting structures it contains. It is conversational, though not always in an easy way. This place challenges me, encourages me to deconstruct, analyse, reflect and reconstruct and it provides opportunities for social enrichment of my learning experiences. Of course, my personal learning space also allows me to create multiple eportfolios for myriad purposes and diverse audiences.*

I'd suggest that such a description still holds up, though we would place more emphasis on the scaffolding, the support and the surfacing of learning that is evident through so many of these case studies.

In her 2012 'Bash book introduction Alison Poot (now our Chief Customer Officer) followed up her observation that *most of our customers went in search of an 'eportfolio' and then ended up with PebblePad* with an insight that really speaks to the nature of this tool:

> *It is only in PP that users are pushed to make sense of their experiences to a much deeper level through the inbuilt templates and to reflect upon a variety of learning opportunities that might otherwise have gone unnoticed.*

I always think about curiosity as a hallmark of an impactful education, but I suspect there's a very close relationship between curiosity and what is, and isn't, noticed. Professor Colin Beard in his excellent book Experiential Learning Design talks about **developing the habit of noticing**. For me this is such a simple construct, and yet incredibly powerful – and so I'm excited to see across so many of these case studies obvious indications of scaffolding, nudges and supports in place to help students plan (to notice), record (what they noticed) and then reflect (on what they noticed) to make sense of the experience. As I heard on a recent trip to North America, helping to squeeze every drop of learning value from the experiential sponge!

Our 2014 PebbleBash was themed around learning design. We have always been careful to limit our claims for how wonderful PebblePad is. Of course, it is pretty good as a personal learning platform. It promotes curiosity and understanding through the inbuilt templates (it helps you *notice*), it provides powerful tools for educators to design their own templates, it has tools to track, evidence and view developing capability, it celebrates creativity and individual storytelling through its portfolios and pages, and allows journaling through its blogs and logs - but it has always been the case that the very best uses of PebblePad arise from thoughtful learning design. Great design typically embraces assessment as a powerful learning opportunity, leverages the power of other stakeholders in the process, and is at its core learner- and learning-centric.

Colin (Dalziel – my co-conspirator and co-founder)'s introduction in 2014 asserted that assessment is arguably the most powerful driver for learner engagement. *Good learning design with well aligned assessment, should result in assessment processes that don't just test the learning but support and enhance it.*

Assessment clearly remains important to our community, with 14 case studies linking the theme of **Authentic Assessment** to their work. Colin went on to comment on the value of surfacing the process, making not just the final outcomes of an activity apparent, but also enabling students to highlight the learning journey they have undertaken. With concerns about essay mills, and contract cheating now eclipsed by AI-alarm, it is more important than ever that the process of learning is surfaced – made visible for those assessing the work, but also so that learners can see and make sense of the things they did, and the skills they learned when undertaking a task. The value of surfacing that learning is clearly evident through multiple case studies in this book.

As this is our 20th anniversary it is perhaps also worth reprising Colin's brief history lesson from the 2014 introduction:

> *The coding started in early April 2004, making PebbleBash 2014 almost 10 years to the day after the first few lines of code were written and the first features started to appear. With just 3 people working on the development we somehow managed to get a version ready for 160 students to pilot at the University of Wolverhampton by the 1st of October.*

As I recall, it took Colin almost as long to write his introduction as it did for us to build the first version of PebblePad! Joking aside, it is incredible that we have been doing this for 20 years, and that the case studies gathered in this book add further to our understanding of the incredible body of practice that has developed over this time.

2016 saw the focus of the 'Bash shift to **Future Readiness**, and as a theme its importance has only grown over the last eight years. As I wrote in that year's 'Bash book introduction:

> *The world is increasingly complex, connected and collaborative. The currency of content knowledge is diminishing. Our focus is upon knowing how, and knowing why - above and beyond knowing what.*

Nine of this year's case studies concern themselves either wholly or in part with this theme, though in the way we now organise our, or rather **your**, work, this theme is **Employable and Future Ready**.

Thanks to the various calamities wrought by the pandemic, 2018 turned out to be our last face-to-face international 'Bash before this anniversary gathering. It was themed around **The Enterprise Endeavour** and reflected the growing number of campus-wide initiatives and/or those institutions where PebblePad was widely used across multiple disciplines and by multiple faculties and departments. Those examples of widescale use have continued to grow, increasingly as a result of the kinds of curriculum reimagining or transformation celebrated at this PebbleBash, and expertly addressed by our keynote speakers.

Segueing from keynotes to other kinds of special speaker (though of course, you are all special to us) I'd like to make extra special mention of Jenny Masters, an early and enthusiastic PebblePad advocate in Australia, a presenter at our very first PebbleBash – and presenting 14 years later at this 2024 'Bash. Jenny was referenced in the introduction to the 2018 'Bash book, stressing the importance of careful planning – another theme emerging from this year's case studies.

She provided us with a useful metaphor to describe the process of implementation:

- The road to Portfolio Utopia is long and there will be bumps, obstacles and wrong turns as we go.
- The role of driver is important, but so too is that of the navigator; it is important to know where you are going.
- There isn't much point in reaching a destination if you lose your passengers along the way.
- It certainly helps to have a reliable vehicle to successfully negotiate the terrain.

One of the lasting consequences of the 2018 'Bash was the impromptu conversation we had with the assembled delegates – debating the perennial question about what PebblePad was! From that conversation came our most current, and so far our longest lasting definition – **PebblePad: the learning journey platform**. From that came our re-interpretation of the original learning journey diagram and the emergence of the themes and streams that provide the conceptual glue that holds this book, and this conference together:

- Authentic Assessment
- Flexible Learning Design
- Belonging and Wellbeing
- Employable and Future Ready
- Professional Identity and Capability

And so, I suppose, to conclude this introduction – before it becomes a chapter in its own right! – I can do no better than to draw upon the words Alison Poot used when crafting an abridged introduction to the 'Bash book of the 'Bash that never was in 2020:

> Each time we plan for a conference I am asked if I would like to hand over the editorial reins. Each time I resist because I derive so much pleasure from being the first to read the new wave of stories – a bit like opening a series of gifts, full of anticipation for what is inside.
>
> Every year I am surprised, delighted and inspired by the innovation and great practice to be found within, and I love recognizing the echoes of the foundations of others' work from previous years.

Despite the extra-ordinarily tight fiscal conditions that face so many institutions and individuals in higher education across the world, for this 20th Anniversary PebbleBash we are blessed with *gifts* from around the globe. From Tasmania on the edge of the Great Southern Ocean, to an impressive contingent of *paddlers* from either side of the border in the Pacific North West. From Ohio, Ontario and Ormskirk, from across the UK and across the world, old friends and colleagues – and shiny new ones, we are thrilled to represent your work in this conference book, and to have so many of you join us in Edinburgh.

Why re-invent the wheel when you can draw upon the inspiration of others? Surely the very point of this book, and of this conference! From a chap called Shane, writing in 2018:

> I have really enjoyed reading these case studies, I am excited about discovering even more from the presentations that I am able to attend during the conference. Most of all I am anxious to learn as much as possible from the combined wisdom of our wonderful PebblePad community to help us ensure that our unique personal learning platform remains future ready for everything you plan to throw at it.

I wish you all a fabulous conference, and for those who were unable to make it, I hope this book will help you think of new and exciting ways to use PebblePad in your own practice, and with your own learners.

All the very best with your innovating and risk-taking.

Shane
Founder I CEO I CMM
June 2024

Supporting the Ambitions of Higher Education

∽

Peer Reviewed Research Paper

1

Introducing PebblePad from the ground up: It's a bumpy road to the top

Peter Kilgour[1], Kevin Petrie[1], & Carole Hunter[2]
[1]Education, Avondale University, Australia
[2]PebblePad Australia

Abstract

This study traces the introduction of PebblePad to the learning and teaching practices of a small university. Originating from a single academic's vision for its potential use, PebblePad has been slowly adopted across other disciplines through localised participatory leadership. The way this process developed presents an opportunity to explore participants' perspectives on ground up change management in the development of PebblePad into the learning and teaching pedagogy of a small university. Being introduced by a single academic in the teacher education discipline and slowly adopted across other faculties, ideas of change management from both management and pedagogical perspectives are presented as a unique case where change does not emanate from the management level. Five staff members were interviewed about their introduction and experiences with PebblePad. The results demonstrated that the participants appreciated the training from PebblePad and the collegial support of their peer academics. While mentioning the issue of time management and technology fatigue in learning another innovation, it was accepted that the ground up approach was appropriate because of the demonstrated effectiveness of the new application and the low-pressure mode of adoption.

Keywords

Change management; pedagogy; information technology; eportfolio;

Introduction

Despite a history dating back to 1897, Avondale University (AU) is one of Australia's newest universities. The University focuses on an exceptional quality of experience within a limited range of disciplines, including business, teaching, nursing, outdoor leadership, counselling, and theology.

As for all Australian universities, partnerships with a variety of comparable institutions for benchmarking purposes is a regular part of teaching practices at AU, and occasionally this can lead to insights that are incorporated into the University. In 2019, the first author was involved in a partnership with the University of Tasmania using common assessments of pre-service teacher placements. As part of this process, he became aware of PebblePad as a powerful and valuable system for planning and documenting placement experiences in an authentic and safe way. However, it was clear it had a much broader use beyond placements for authentic learning and assessment more generally, and he was keen for colleagues across disciplines at his own institution to discover the same benefits. This study traces the introduction and adoption of PebblePad into AU from those beginnings.

Background

While technologies are often introduced in higher education institutions through a top-down initiative (Mansaray, 2019) this is not always the case. Many institutions have processes whereby individuals can request support to pilot new technologies, evaluating their use for wider adoption. In other cases, schools/faculties may identify a technology that meets a discipline-specific pedagogical need and then purchase licences independently. Regardless of origin, these 'ground up' strategies (Laig & Abocejo, 2021) do not neatly fit into traditional change management models (Hiatt & Creasey, 2003; Kotter, 2007) that often assume the incorporation of defined outcomes, powerful change advocates, and formal reinforcement and support. Instead, processes are often sporadic and emergent, relying on internal motivations and favourable contextual factors that encourage uptake in the absence of formal support.

For those initiating technologies outside of formal change initiatives, there can be a dual set of challenges:

- **Managing up**, by convincing those with managerial, IT and financial authority to formally support emerging use; and
- **Spreading across**, by encouraging rhizomatic expansion of usage through pedagogical connection, influence and impact (Deleuze & Guattari, 1988) .

These challenges are usually taken on without resourcing – either financially or via workload, driven largely by a deep belief in the value of the technology for enhancing the learning and teaching process. While the 'spreading across' challenge can continue at either a fast or slow pace, to become sustainable the 'managing up' challenge must be met, ensuring the initiative is both aligned with broader learning and teaching strategies and accompanied by pedagogical and technological support to engage those beyond the early adopters.

This study represents an initial exploration of the experiences of academics who collaborated with the first author as part of this ground up strategy, some of whom were enthusiastic and others more reluctant. It attempts to explore the pedagogical and technological rationales behind decisions to move ahead with PebblePad, and the role the ground up strategy played in these individual decisions. It is also an exploration of how one institution has moved from an individual champion to broader adoption and managerial engagement and support of PebblePad, and the insights gained from this experience.

Bringing these factors together is our research question:

What is the experience of one tertiary institution where one academic staff member seeks to assimilate innovation (PebblePad) across the institution?

Literature

Pedagogy, technology, and the nature of educational change

A 'pedagogy-first' approach to educational change has a strong history in higher education, often pushing against the promises of new technologies to transform learning. Yet as Fawns (2022) argues, the relationship between technology and pedagogy is much more 'entangled' than either of these narratives might suggest. A more realistic view would see teachers, designers, students, and other stakeholders all playing their part alongside purpose, context, values, methods and technology in a complex, relational 'dance' where outcomes emerge over time. In turn, he suggests that understanding a technology depends on understanding the local culture and infrastructure, and how various stakeholders understand each technology within their own contexts.

Hunter and Dunham (2023) reference these entanglements and 'messy' interrelationships in the context of the broader learning ecosystem and the role of capability builders within it. They draw on rhizomatic thinking (Deleuze & Guattari, 1987) to describe the constant, open-ended nature of change within this ecosystem, contrasting this to the linear change trajectories we often expect of top-down change management initiatives. Through this lens, change is driven by complex connections, influence, and impact. New connections can lead to 'ruptures' or opportunities to branch out while remaining connected to core. These ruptures allow for growth and the spread of change in often unexpected directions, stimulated by individual experiences and needs. This kind of opportunistic rhizomatic change can pave the way for larger pedagogical shifts and aspirations that may require deeper planning and/or managerial engagement.

Factors affecting technology adoption

Without the support of a strategy, leadership and a broader vision, technology adoption via ground up change relies even more heavily on individual factors. New connections create ruptures signalling opportunities for growth and change, but a myriad of factors moderate whether those opportunities will ultimately be taken up.

Various models have been developed to predict whether individuals will adopt new technologies. At a broad level, the Technology Acceptance Model (Davis, 1989) proposes that two factors influence technology adoption: whether the user perceives it to be useful and whether it's perceived to be easy to use, each of which has a set of antecedents. External factors (e.g. technology design) influence these perceptions, which lead to an affective response, or inclination to use the technology.

A more nuanced predictive model - the Unified Theory of Acceptance and Use of Technology (UTAUT) - was developed by Venkatesh et al. (2003). This model includes four direct and four moderating constructs that are asserted to influence adoption. The direct constructs are the level to which the user expects the technology to improve their performance (performance expectancy) and reduce the effort they need to complete the task (effort expectancy), as well as whether it has been recommended by valued others (social influence), and the level of support provided (facilitating conditions). The moderating factors include gender, age, previous experience and whether the use is voluntary or not.

Adapting the Kegan and Lahey (2001) approach to overcoming resistance to change, Table 1 considers the direct constructs in UTAUT and how they might be supported by a single person with limited authority promoting technology adoption. It should also be noted that amongst the moderating factors, ground up approaches naturally support voluntary uptake.

Table 1: UTAUT predictors for adoption and associated strategies

Predictor	Strategies to support adoption	Ground up strategies adopted at AU
Performance expectancy	Education and communication	Small demonstrations focusing on outcome improvements at learning and teaching events, visiting people in their offices as a 'peer with an idea'
Effort expectancy	Education and communication	Shared stories of improved efficiencies, entry-level demonstrations of simple functionality linked to real and immediate outcomes
Social influence	Participation and involvement	Being involved and making recommendations as a colleague to create a network of motivated supporters
Facilitating conditions	Local support at point of need	Organising training and encouraging participation across disciplines, being on call for support and 'checking in' on progress

Sorensen and Sarjeant-Jenkins (2016) observe that planning at 'grassroots' level assists employees in seeing the relevance to their discipline area. They note that while a management directive to implement a new initiative would be interpreted as a whole of institution initiative, an initiative introduced at the 'peer' level would normally be more discipline-focused and therefore seen as more relevant.

The higher education context and the nature of specific educational technologies may have an added influence on technology adoption. For example, fear of failure, time pressures, and competing commitments (Kegan and Lahey, 2001) are all highly relevant factors leading to resistance in the context of higher education. In addition, as a system founded on student-centred learning, PebblePad's underlying philosophy, reflected in its system design, challenges traditional ways of teaching and so may require users to cross a number of threshold concepts related to online teaching (Kilgour et al., 2018; Northcote et al., 2017) or their pedagogical philosophy (Powell & Kusuma-Powell, 2015). Threshold concepts are gateways or hurdles that the learner needs to cross before the next stage of learning or application can proceed. Similarly, Alder (2010) suggests that learning is based on patterns and where a new initiative or concept is introduced, new patterns need to be formed which may mean breaking old patterns or integrating new patterns into the old ones. Powell and Kusuma-Powell (2015) refer to these as 'adaptive challenges', requiring a changed mindset whereby teachers "rethink our deeply held values, beliefs, assumptions, and even our professional identity" (p. 67).

Participatory leadership from the ground up

While much of the literature focuses on change *management*, this needs to be distinguished from change *leadership*, which is generally understood to be more people-focused and relies on influence to enable change. In higher education, real pedagogical change can occur at macro, meso and micro-levels through the big and small actions of many people (Childs et al., 2013). Indeed, the recent Advance HE Report has found that more distributed models of leadership that extend across these levels are essential for achieving desired outcomes and culture (Johns, 2023)

At the micro-level, participatory leadership approaches which emphasise involvement, collaboration, sharing practice and leading by example are valuable. These approaches can foster enhanced engagement, trust and empowerment, strong commitment, and improved learning and innovation (Kezar & Holcombe, 2017). This more informal, situated approach to leadership can also be adapted to individual context, needs and learning approaches. Indeed, micro-leaders can be powerful initiators of change in university settings, creating "interest, enthusiasm and unparalleled momentum for an innovation at a local level" (Childs et al., 2013, p. 38). This is critical in a context where academics value their autonomy.

Yet for ground up initiatives to attract the levels of support needed to ensure sustainability, links will ultimately need to be established with those who have responsibility for fostering institution-wide implementation. In 'managing up', it can help to consider incentives for management to support ground-up initiatives. This may include perceived outcomes and efficiencies (e.g. from the move from paper to digital), alignment with learning and teaching strategies, and financial considerations (Hamel, 2009). A ground-up initiative can be a rich space for gathering information around the real experiences and impacts of a technology for presentation to decision-makers.

Methods

A phenomenological qualitative research design was implemented to include the experiences of those involved with introducing PebblePad into their pedagogy. The themes explored revolved firstly around the way participants were introduced to PebblePad, and secondly whether PebblePad changed their approach to the pedagogy they used in their units.

The use of phenomenological qualitative research to examine lecturers' attitudes and perceptions towards the change management process of implementing PebblePad at AU was found to be well suited to studying emotional and affective human experiences (Merriam & Tisdell, 2015). This method helped the researchers gain a picture of individuals' lived experiences (Mayoh & Onwuegbuzie, 2015). By using this design, we were able to lay aside any predetermined understandings and authentically explore these experiences (Flynn & Korcuska, 2018).

Data were collected using one-to-one recorded interviews conducted by a lecturer who had not taken part in the early stages of PebblePad usage to ensure there were no pre-conceived notions or conflicts of interest. The interviews were semi-structured (Adams,

2015) where potential guiding questions were proposed, but the conversation was permitted to go in other directions provided it contributed to the main aims of the study.

Purposive sampling (Etikan et al., 2016) was used to identify five participants to be interviewed who fitted the inclusion criteria. These criteria included current staff members at AU who had been: employed at AU for at least two years; working in an area where PebblePad was being adopted into the workflow; participating in PebblePad training; either an early adopter or demonstrated some reluctance to adopt; and agreed to participate.

The key aim of the interviews was to explore the motivation of staff to implement PebblePad in their area and to report on their lived experience of the change process required to implement PebblePad in their discipline. The interviews were designed to seek staff reflections on the pedagogical positives and/or negatives of implementing PebblePad and their perceptions about the implementation process in terms of change management at AU.

The data from the interviews were transcribed and inductive thematic analysis (Guest et al., 2011) was used to derive meaning with no preconceptions of what the outcomes may be.

Results

All five interviewees were staff of AU and had experience using PebblePad. Three were academic staff members, one a member of the professional staff supporting the use of PebblePad within their school, and the fifth a learning designer supporting the use of PebblePad across the university.

The interviewees provided responses on several themes including enablers and inhibitors to the introduction of PebblePad, change management observations, and perceptions of ground-up vs top-down approaches to implementing initiatives at AU.

This section will firstly examine those aspects that participants identified as being enablers to the introduction and implementation of PebblePad in their area. Three themes were identified as being significant: technical and pedagogical support; practical benefits specific to discipline area; and the lack of 'pressure' in the implementation process.

Technical and pedagogical support

All participants spoke positively of the support they received in considering PebblePad as a viable tool for their area. The initial introduction for each participant was the enthusiasm of an AU staff member who had trialled PebblePad and who shared positively about its potential. As one participant enumerated, *"one of the big enablers of course is the advocates who already ... have found it useful ... and therefore can really intelligently articulate how it's been useful for them..."*. This initial introduction led to an opportunity to attend a training session run by PebblePad, with the presenter being described as *"very easy to get along with and supportive"* providing *"a good foundation to deciding on the product ... the capabilities of the product"*. Staff valued that this introductory session was tailored for the group in attendance and was seen as a *"very useful thing in terms of raising awareness, showing people not to be scared of it and putting it together in a format that they could go to and look at later".*

The ongoing support was likewise seen as vital to the eventual uptake within their discipline area. Some of this support was from the local staff member who had championed the use of PebblePad and who was seen as happy to be called on to provide advice and support, being described as *"patient and persevering"*. One participant however sounded a note of caution, suggesting that they were sometimes reticent to 'annoy' someone who had taken this on voluntarily and who was providing this support above and beyond their normal workload. They felt they would be more likely to reach out for help if it was someone who had been assigned this 'help-role' by management: *"I get really conscious of the fact that I'm relying heavily on the local school champion at the beginning of semesters"*. However, it was acknowledged that without this 'local' level of support they would have been unlikely to continue implementation, a view shared by another participant.

The ongoing support from the PebblePad representative received positive endorsement, with participants finding AU's liaison *"very helpful as the go-to person for assistance ... whenever we hit something that we get a little bit stuck with"*. Participants found that they had received the *"proper training and ... received the proper support that we needed"* and that this was *"a good foundation to the whole thing becoming to what we are today ... and we still have that support from PebblePad"*. Responsiveness was seen as a key factor to persevering with PebblePad during the learning journey: *"She was amazing ... we could just email at any time and depending on the time changes, and just ask questions. Say, look, we need help. Can we get a Zoom? ... I [would] just email her and she would get straight on [to it]"*.

Multiple participants noted the importance of the online resources that were created, enabling staff to engage with the learning material in their own time and at their own pace. In commenting on the importance of this aspect, one participant suggested: *"I don't think people want to be a burden ... they don't necessarily want to keep pestering people. They don't want to feel like they're foolish or incapable."*

Practical applications and benefits

All participants emphasised the importance of seeing the benefits specific to their area. *"You see the potential, you see how it's genuinely going to benefit your students, especially given that these days we're really trying to push reflective practice. So for me, that was my buy-in, that was my enabler, was seeing the relevance"*. Another added; *"I actually saw it as being very useful for a lot of the units that I teach, which are so portfolio driven"*, and from someone in a different discipline: *"It was soon [I] realised that, oh, actually this makes my job easier and it gives me a little bit more time"*.

Participants appreciated that the training and the support offered was discipline specific and that they were given the opportunity to see how other universities were benefiting from this. *"You could collaboratively get together with other people in your specialty field out of your university, just to inspire as well. That was actually an advantage."* As one person emphasised: *"The initial buy-in has to be because you personally feel excited"*.

It is useful to note the importance of people being very clear on what they wanted PebblePad to achieve for them, as one individual commented: *"I think what was an advantage and enabler ... was that we actually had very clear goals in what we wanted to use it for."* Two participants emphasised the need for awareness as to what the technology is designed to do well, one noting that *"[where] it gets difficult is where it tries to be used for other purposes where that's not what its core design was for".*

The practical benefits were seen as greatest when the technology played to its strengths:

> *"... if you're using PebblePad in your lecturing or as an assessment, just because you think you should be using PebblePad ... then [that] becomes quite distracting and it's almost like busy work. And it can take you, the lecturer, a huge amount of effort to massage something that doesn't fit PebblePad into PebblePad".*

> *"I think it's been marketed to sort of have a little bit more ... applications than it probably was originally designed for, which I think therefore might make it a little bit confusing to people who are new to it".*

Two of the participants emphasised the importance of pedagogy driving technology, rather than the other way around.

Lack of pressure

Being a grassroots driven initiative meant there was not the implementation pressure usually associated with a top-down change management approach. *"We weren't forced to do it because we weren't forced to take it on board,"* one person enumerated. Another highlighted that they felt this was important in ensuring their creativity and curiosity was engaged in the process: *"And so coming from that, without this thing that's imposed, I felt free to just go where my creativity and imagination took me. I think it's just been this natural, organic, comfortable, I can have a go at this because I don't have to, but it looks good, so I'm going to try".*

One participant commented at greater length on the benefits of a ground up level approach to this type of implementation: *"I think too, academic/teachers, the way I've mostly experienced them, tend to react better to the organically introduced as opposed to the, 'you have to do this'. Because again, I've seen several examples of that ... But specific to PebblePad, I think it is one of those things that really is more successful when introduced organically, when people are given that more autonomy to how if they want to use it and how they might want to go about introducing it to their teaching perhaps".*

Some even felt motivated by the 'fear of missing out'. As one person commented, *"the fear of missing out type thing, which I think ... probably, affects things like PebblePad ... 'Oh, I've heard this PebblePad thing. Oh, I better look at that. I don't know about that. Should I be using that?'"*

A couple of participants also connected this area to that of institutional culture, with one commenting: *"I think just creating that culture of trying things and not being roasted if it doesn't work."* They found this indicative of the area in which they worked, and in general felt safe to experiment and try new things in their school without fear of failure.

Barriers to implementing PebblePad

In commenting on barriers to the introduction of PebblePad at AU, the two most significant themes were that of technical barriers and time barriers, with strong overlap between these two. However, while all participants raised the issue of 'time' as a significant consideration, not all felt that the technology itself was a barrier, with two of the interviewees feeling the platform was user-friendly and intuitive. Three of the participants emphasised the learning curve needed to master the platform. *"It was pretty clunky actually. It was pretty technical to get it figured out. So if it hadn't have been for Justin, I would've just thrown my hands up in the air and said, I just can't work with this thing."*

This theme was echoed by others: *"I feel it's not immediately an easy thing to come to grasps with. It does seem to be a difficult thing to get your head around the way it works"* or from another participant: *"I don't think it's an intuitive thing to learn for both staff and students. I think they find it probably just as challenging for some aspects of the work."*

One participant emphasised the challenge of *"technology fatigue"*: *"And I think that that's there with a lot of technologies because of just the relentless sort of ... technology fatigue. [There is] stuff that's just being thrown at all educators, and some of it good, some of it bad, some of it genuinely helpful and designed to be helpful and others genuinely designed just to make money out of an unsuspecting industry that just thinks that they need to keep up ... just that very factor of do we do things just because we think, 'Wow, we better be part of that. We should buy one of them because we don't have one".*

The need to ensure that student voice was integral to the process was also noted and that their buy-in was factored. One discipline area intentionally surveyed their students regarding the use of PebblePad, adjusting the following year in response to this feedback.

Another school reported 'student buy-in' as a barrier in one of the teaching units, leading the lecturer to comment: *"It's almost like the students really need to be canvassed about what works for them rather than us coming up with grand ideas and imposing upon the students".* However, overall participants reported a positive response from most students who were comfortable and supportive with the use of technology when engaging with assessment tasks.

Time barriers

As might be expected, the theme of being time-poor was a consistent one: *"Yes, so many things, and we [are] stretched to the limit with, and our brains are stretched and we are emotionally tired from all the things. So, on the one hand, it is just another thing."* Or as another commented: *"I have also observed those who it is just too much on top of what they have, and they've got various reasons for feeling that way. And so for them, it's been a much harder uptake because it is. You do have to get your head around it, and if you are feeling tired or stretched to the max, it's very hard to invest the mental energy".*

It was noted by one participant that *"the biggest barrier was just our lack of knowledge initially of what was involved. It wasn't just creating, it was then implementing, and the management side of it, but it was probably our naivety about the program itself"*.

To assist in managing this 'fear of the unknown', one School within AU designed a pilot trial of PebblePad for the assessment task they were hoping to implement first. *"So while the rest of the students used the paper-based, we decided to use about 10 or 12 students as a test run to see how we would manage things ... we decided to go with a small cohort of students to minimise risk because if this was something that could not be reverted, then it would've been a logistical problem"*.

Following a successful trial, the discipline designed an implementation plan particular to their area, considering learnings from the trial along with the needs of the staff. This included managing the time-barriers and to ensure the implementation was 'fit for purpose' within their area.

Pedagogical considerations

Interestingly, no mention was made by any of the five participants of pedagogical considerations as a barrier. *"I see PebblePad as a genuine authentic assessment tool ... very helpful in that space,"* wrote one. *"It's a great tool for those reflective learning journal type situations where you want to be capturing the students."* Or as another commented, *"it was a really more efficient way of getting across the skills"*. It is possible that the efforts to develop stronger pedagogical underpinnings initiated by AU's Centre for the Advancement of Learning & Teaching (CASTL) over the past few years has resulted in a shared understanding that facilitates this acceptance. It is also likely that the practical way in which PebblePad was introduced resulted in staff gaining a clear and early view of the potential pedagogical benefits.

Discussion

The main purpose of this paper is to report a case study of a small university (AU) that adopted PebblePad using a 'ground-up' approach to facilitate the change. Academic and professional staff were interviewed to compare their individual experiences of technology adoption to the theory and literature of change management where new technology is involved.

While several themes emerged from the interview phase of this study, it should be noted that as highlighted by Fawns (2022), there is a strong connection (referred to as 'entanglement') between the themes, and it should not be assumed that the aspects of technology and pedagogy can be separated entirely. For example, the ideas of *technology fatigue* and *time pressure* reported by our participants are related to pedagogy in the sense that as Venkatesh et al. (2003) explain, there is a need to balance 'effort expectancy' against the reality of possible saved time because of the pedagogical advantages of the innovation.

Examining the advantages and disadvantages of using a 'ground up' approach, our participants confirmed that within the changing learning environment, it was helpful to have a 'capacity builder' (Hunter & Dunham, 2023) who was a colleague and a constant non-threatening source of support.

Further supporting the advantages of a ground up approach, Kegan and Lahey (2001) discuss the idea of working with colleagues or a 'peer with an idea' and note that the introduction of an innovation can benefit from a relaxed approach where casual 'drop-ins' of a support colleague can work the best. Our participants reported that the lack of pressure to adopt and use PebblePad was an advantage in the implementation phase.

The Technology Acceptance Model (Davis, 1989) mentioned earlier identifies the two properties of new technology that determine its level of acceptance. These are the usefulness of the application and its ease of use. Both are relevant in our results. It was generally accepted that PebblePad is a useful and practical innovation. No respondent questioned its potential to enhance their pedagogy. Not everybody however found it straight forward or intuitive to learn. It must be concluded that the benefits of PebblePad they enthusiastically reported made the learning hurdle worth pursuing.

One of the strong result themes is the importance of 'relevance' to the discipline area. As pointed out by (Sorensen & Sarjeant-Jenkins, 2016), individuals (and schools) are not looking so much to benefits for the organisation as a whole, but rather to how this is relevant and beneficial to their particular area. Our participants answered questions in the context of their own discipline and were eager to translate the benefits espoused by the local champion into their own domain.

Conclusion

This case study of PebblePad adoption from the ground up has demonstrated many of the advantages in having a person on staff who believes in an innovation and uses it in their own pedagogy. It confirms the literature that when a colleague who is relaxed and supportive, yet an enthusiastic champion of an innovation works with those who would likewise benefit from the application, technology adoption is more likely to be embraced (Kegan & Lahey, 2001).

Surprisingly, no questions were raised over the new pedagogy of PebblePad, with the participants accepting its numerous benefits for learning and assessment but as expected, the normal issues of time allocation and hesitation at facing 'another innovation' were part of this study.

This study confirmed that the issues of fear of new technology, pedagogy and management cannot be siloed, but needs to be considered together when introducing a new tool.

The overall finding from this study highlights the value of initial micro-leadership in building momentum for technology adoption. From the initial introduction of PebblePad by one academic, and the low-key encouragement and support given to their colleagues, its use has spread across the disciplines and has been adopted as part of AU's 21st Century learning and teaching model by its Centre for the Advancement of Teaching and Learning (CASTL).
References

References

Adams, W. C. (2015). Conducting semi-structured interviews. *Handbook of practical program evaluation*, 492-505.

Alder, A. (2010). *Pattern Making, Pattern Breaking: Using Past Experience and New Behaviour in Training, Education and Change Management.* Gower Publishing, Ltd.

Childs, M., Brown, M., Keppell, M., Nicholas, Z., Hunter, C., & Hard, N. (2013). Managing institutional change through distributive leadership approaches: engaging academics and teaching support staff in blended and flexible learning.

Davis, F. D. (1989). Perceived usefulness, perceived ease of use, and user acceptance of information technology. *MIS quarterly*, 319-340.

Deleuze, G., & Guattari, F. (1988). *A thousand plateaus: Capitalism and schizophrenia.* Bloomsbury Publishing.

Etikan, I., Musa, S. A., & Alkassim, R. S. (2016). Comparison of convenience sampling and purposive sampling. *American journal of theoretical and applied statistics, 5(1)*, 1-4.

Fawns, T. (2022). An entangled pedagogy: Looking beyond the pedagogy—technology dichotomy. *Postdigital Science and Education, 4(3)*, 711-728.

Flynn, S. V., & Korcuska, J. S. (2018). Credible phenomenological research: A mixed-methods study. *Counselor Education and Supervision, 57(1)*, 34-50.

Guest, G., MacQueen, K. M., & Namey, E. E. (2011). *Applied thematic analysis.* Sage publications.

Hamel, G. (2009). Moon shots for management. *Harvard business review, 87(2)*, 91-98.

Hiatt, J., & Creasey, T. J. (2003). Change management: *The people side of change.* Prosci.

Hunter, C., & Dunham, N. (2023). Partnering through the plateau: A rhizomatic exploration of digital capability building. (*in preparation*), 2023.

Johns, A. (2023). New demands on universities and their people will require fresh thinking on professional development.
https://wonkhe.com/blogs/new-demands-on-universities-and-their-people-will-require-fresh-thinking-on-professional-development/

Kegan, R., & Lahey, L. L. (2001). *The real reason people won't change.* Harvard Business Review Boston, MA.

Kezar, A. J., & Holcombe, E. M. (2017). Shared leadership in higher education. *Washington, DC: American Council on Education*, 1-36.

Kilgour, P., Reynaud, D., Northcote, M., McLoughlin, C., & Gosselin, K. P. (2018). Threshold concepts about online pedagogy for novice online teachers in higher education. *Higher Education Research & Development*, 1-15.

Kotter, J. P. (2007). Leading change: Why transformation efforts fail.

Laig, R. B. D., & Abocejo, F. T. (2021). Change management process in a mining company: Kotter's 8-Step change model. *Journal of Management, Economics, and Industrial Organization, 5(3)*, 31-50.

Mansaray, H. E. (2019). The role of leadership style in organisational change management: a literature review. *Journal of Human Resource Management, 7(1)*, 18-31.

Mayoh, J., & Onwuegbuzie, A. J. (2015). Toward a conceptualization of mixed methods phenomenological research. *Journal of mixed methods research, 9(1)*, 91-107.

Merriam, S. B., & Tisdell, E. J. (2015). *Qualitative research: A guide to design and implementation.* John Wiley & Sons.

Northcote, M. T., Gosselin, K. P., Kilgour, P. W., McLoughlin, C., & Boddey, C. (2017). Using threshold concepts about online teaching to support novice online teachers: Designing professional development guidelines to individually assist academic staff ("me") and collectively guide the institution ("us").

Powell, W., & Kusuma-Powell, O. (2015). Overcoming resistance to new ideas. *Phi Delta Kappan, 96(8)*, 66-69.

Sorensen, C., & Sarjeant-Jenkins, R. (2016). Sustainable growth with sustainable resources: Using change management, participative consultation, and grassroots planning for a new future. *Library Management, 37(3)*, 114-124.

Venkatesh, V., Morris, M., Davis, G., & Davis, F. (2003). User acceptance of information technology: towards a unified view. Manag Inf Syst Q 27: 425–478. In.

Case Studies

2

Reimagining eportfolios for learning and employment: A case study in Interior Design

Hailey Bassiri[1], Hailey Bell[1], Paola Gavilanez[2] & Gillian Sudlow[3]
[1]Student, Wilson School of Design, Kwantlen Polytechnic University, CA
[2]Wilson School of Design, Kwantlen Polytechnic University, CA
[3]Teaching and Learning Commons, Kwantlen Polytechnic University, CA

The Context

Kwantlen Polytechnic University (KPU) in Vancouver, Canada is strategically incorporating eportfolios as a high-impact practice to achieve goals established in its academic plan. The American Association of Colleges and Universities (AAC&U) recognizes eportfolios as such (Watson, et al., 2016) and KPU's Academic Plan outlines several of these goals related to eportfolio integration (KPU, n.d.). One goal focuses on enhancing student success through rigorous curricula, teaching excellence, and dedicated support systems. This includes preparing students to think and act independently, possess strong digital and technological skills, and demonstrate a capacity for integrated thinking. A second goal specifically emphasizes embedding and enhancing eportfolios that reflect open education strategies and appreciate the added value of eportfolio practices.

KPU is committed to promoting eportfolio pedagogy across the institution through the use of PebblePad as a platform. The Teaching and Learning department (T&L) recognizes that PebblePad supports effective pedagogy by helping students articulate what they know, how they know it, and share evidence from their work throughout their programs of study (KPU Teaching and Learning, n.d.).

KPU actively participated in the 2022-2023 AAC&U Institute on ePortfolios, leading to a partnership between T&L and the Wilson School of Design (WSD). The joint project aimed to implement eportfolios across the WSD's seven design programs and to inspire faculty to adopt eportfolios that align with industry standards, meet employer expectations, achieve accreditation requirements, and address goals across programs (Sudlow, n.d.).

In addition to these institutional efforts, faculty and students in the WSD sought to explore the potential of eportfolio pedagogy in design generally, and interior design specifically. Time releases were provided to participating faculty for research that focussed on two main issues:

- Meeting employer expectations by documenting the development of soft skills through eportfolios.
- Leveraging eportfolios for knowledge transfer between courses and years while enhancing the continuity of learning experiences for students within design programs.

The Problem

The first challenge at hand involved addressing limitations in traditional portfolios within the design professions. Digital portfolios in design are standard practice, however, they are traditionally curated, visually-dominant showcase portfolios meant to display a student's best work and various design-related hard skills. Missing is a cohesive reflection of an individual's values and personal narrative. To tackle this, our initial investigation explored the potential of eportfolios to go beyond displaying finished design products, i.e. a showcase portfolio. The question posed was whether employers and applicants would benefit from graduate portfolios highlighting not only hard skills but also soft skills, providing a more holistic view of an individual's capabilities.

Another key issue centered around knowledge transfer within the design pedagogy, which heavily emphasizes the process. Despite faculty's focus on reflection, the documentation and connection of learning beyond the course level were at times lacking from the student perspective, resulting in siloed learning experiences and knowledge being left behind. In response, we envisioned a pedagogically innovative approach: a learning portfolio where students engage in folio thinking to document, connect, and reflect on their learning and design process. Folio thinking is described as the "process of engaging in the collection, organization, reflection and connection that leads to a person's ability to speak intelligently and concisely about one's learning experiences, what they mean and their value, and how their experiences relate to each other." (Suter, 2013).

The question posed here was how to strategically implement reflective practices at crucial points in the interior design curriculum to enhance knowledge retention and facilitate the transfer of skills acquired in different courses. Both challenges aimed for outcomes that would not only improve the overall quality of design portfolios but also foster a more holistic understanding of students' capabilities and promote the integration and retention of knowledge within the design curriculum.

The Approach

Our approach involved a strategic and multi-faceted plan that started with the formation of a team and the development of a comprehensive work outline. The plan included securing funding for student assistants, establishing a network of professional contacts spanning the required design disciplines (fashion, product, interior, and graphic design), and formulating a preliminary questionnaire for conducting interviews.

The primary task of the student assistants was to refine the interview process. Each student undertook a thorough literature review, examining job postings, design competitions, and other relevant materials to identify demanded soft skills for entry-level design positions. Tailored questionnaires were crafted for three distinct interviewee types: Industry, Faculty, and Students. The questions explored a range of aspects, including prior experience with eportfolios, perspectives on soft skills, insights into hiring gaps, thoughts on reflective practice, and strategies for implementing a soft skills-focused portfolio. Over the course of five months, 22 online interviews were conducted, each lasting approximately 30-45 minutes.

Eportfolios and PebblePad emerged as potential solutions to the identified issues. The platform is being strategically piloted within interior design coursework, aligning with key points in the curriculum identified by students and faculty. PebblePad was leveraged to maximize reflective practice and showcase connected learning across courses. Its role will extend beyond documentation, serving as the platform for eportfolios that charts the development of soft skills. These eportfolios, housed on PebblePad, were envisioned as integral components of a graduate's portfolio, potentially serving as the primary showcase or an additional asset for job applications, thereby reinforcing the importance of soft skills in the design profession.

The Results

The outcomes of our intervention revealed the need for a shift in addressing the identified issues. Through our conversations with industry we learned that potential employers in design want to know the "person behind the work," but expect students to articulate their values and demonstrate soft skills through the interview portion of the hiring process, not through their portfolios.

Interviews with students and faculty suggested they would benefit from reflecting on and bringing forward their learning through all four years of the program, revealing a 'red thread' connecting key aspects of their learning in-and-outside of the classroom. Structured student reflection that is goal setting in nature and re-evaluates work based on an internal set of values rather than on comparisons or grades, would improve perceptions of learning over time and enable them to identify and articulate who they are as designers.

The research also identified a lack of standardized reflective practices across design disciplines within the WSD. Consequently, our intervention proposed the introduction of structured reflective practices documented via PebblePad, providing an ideal environment for students to establish their values and articulate them in daily life and discussions with others. We anticipate that our proposal will not only enhance student's self-reflection and identity formation as designers but also facilitate a better career path alignment with their values. This approach not only makes the learning process visible but also enables students to draw crucial connections between courses, across years, and with other aspects of their lives. Ultimately, our work seeks to empower students to better identify career paths, opportunities, and align their values as designers, future employees, and global citizens.

Lessons Learnt

The project uncovered valuable insights and identified several barriers that shaped our learning experience. Initially, designers' preconceived ideas about eportfolios being showcase portfolios online highlighted a crucial gap between design pedagogy goals and industry expectations. Communicating this distinction became pivotal to aligning educational objectives with industry priorities.

One significant barrier was the time constraints faced during the design and implementation phase of research findings. Delays in hiring Student Assistants and team members' external commitments posed challenges, emphasizing the need for streamlined processes and efficient resource allocation in future endeavours.

Another barrier emerged during the early interview phase, revealing a gap in understanding of eportfolio pedagogy. A pre-interview phase for baseline development, together with the creation of supporting materials, such as a design eportfolio example focusing on soft skills, could enhance clarity in subsequent interviews.

Unexpectedly, employers expressed confidence in being able to assess applicant's soft skills during interviews and favoured visually dominant, hard-skills-focused portfolios. This challenged our perceived need for eportfolio implementation in the design curriculum. However, a re-evaluation revealed the importance of students creating learning eportfolios documenting reflections and establishing connections between coursework and personal experiences while in school. This process would enhance the applicant's "narrative," indirectly improving job applications through more compelling showcase portfolios and interview presentations.

In Brief

- Implementation of eportfolios and reflective practices in design education is crucial for shaping learner identity. Eportfolios serve as dynamic tools, allowing students to reflect on the development of attitudes beyond hard skills, and fostering confidence. While employers interviewed did not express significant interest in seeing applicants' soft skills documented in showcase portfolios, it became clear that the process pf creating learning eportfolios can nurture a strong personal narrative and enhance students' ability to expound on it.
- To facilitate knowledge transfer in the interior design curriculum, strategic use of reflective practices at key points is essential. Incorporating signature assignments offers significant opportunities for this purpose, streamlining the process. It is crucial to avoid overwhelming students with excessive assignments, both to prevent burnout and to enhance engagement. Implementing feedback loops addresses potential issues, and maintaining flexibility allows for adaptation and continuous improvement of the overall quality of the curriculum over time.

Feedback

In the initial stages of implementation, positive feedback has already emerged regarding our work. Notably, there is recognition that graduates require the ability to articulate their identity during interviews beyond the hard skills and tangible products showcased in resumes and portfolios. Faculty and students who recognize the value of eportfolios have also emphasized the importance of widely sharing the ongoing research to garner support for our initiatives within the WSD community.

Quotes from interviews highlight the significance of portfolio thinking and the documentation of reflective practices. One participant explained that:

> "... we as human beings need the learning to be evident and explicit in order for it to actually make a difference".

An industry professional added that:

> "… hiring managers are more focused on trying to find out how [the applicant's] brain works, how [they] process things rather than [their] aesthetic or styling".

One participant expressed the view that eportfolios serve as an excellent means to showcase a learner's personality, with a particular emphasis on reflective components, as artificial intelligence can compete with visual elements like renderings and imagery. Another interviewee envisioned a self-reflective process integrated into studio courses:

> "Imagine if you would have a self-reflective process in each studio that would force you to look back at your design process from first year, evaluate it, then bring it back the second year, and then reevaluate where you are at".

This iterative approach would become a confidence-building measure that could potentially alleviate anxiety among learners.

Feedback on PebblePad highlighted concerns about the learning curve associated with a new application. Additionally, some students commented on the graphical and visual limitations of the platform, emphasizing the need for education for users and reviewers to distinguish between showcase and learning portfolios.

References

KPU. (n.d.). Academic Plan 2023. Retrieved from https://www.kpu.ca/vp-academic/academic-plan-2023

KPU Teaching and Learning. (n.d.). *PebblePad*. Retrieved from https://www.kpu.ca/teaching-and-learning/technology/pebblepad

Sudlow, G. (n.d.). *KPU team joins AAC&U eportfolio Institute 2022-2023*. ePortfolio Matters KPU. https://wordpress.kpu.ca/eportfolio-matters/matters-of-interest/kpu-team-joins-aacu-eportfolio-institute-2022-2023/

Suter, V., Folio thinking. (2013, June 17). Retrieved January 26, 2024, from https://vsuter.org/eportfolios/

Watson, C. E., Kuh, G. D., Rhodes, T., Penny Light, T., & Chen, H. (2016). Editorial: eportfolios – The Eleventh High Impact Practice. *International Journal of Eportfolio, 6(2)*, 65–69. http://www.theijep.com

3

Creative portfolios and developmental trackers: Use of PebblePad in the School of Education at The University of Sheffield

Hadrian Cawthorne & Cat Bazela
School of Education, University of Sheffield, UK

The Context

The School of Education at the University of Sheffield offers a diverse range of academic and vocational programmes such as Bachelor and Masters degrees in Education, Educational Psychology, Teacher Training, and taught Doctorates in Educational Child Psychology and Education.

As part of the University of Sheffield's Vision and Strategic Plan: Education Pillar, the University is committed to developing a digital strategy that will look to "enhance the student experience through active learning environments, allowing students to connect with information and knowledge in inclusive personalised digital spaces bridging the gap between physical and virtual" (University of Sheffield, 2023b). This involves delivering a rich digital teaching and learning environment which includes providing students with technology that is pedagogically driven and meets the needs of the course. This is echoed in the School of Education's approach to learning and teaching by providing students with a rich digital experience across their courses and programmes.

Within such diverse programmes that span both academic and professional development, we saw the opportunity to enhance the student experience in many ways through the use of PebblePad, due to the flexibility and versatility of the system which allows for customised eportfolios for our students (PebblePad, ndA).

Prior to implementing PebblePad, the School of Education already provided students with a wide range of assessment formats such as essays, presentations, video, and audio. While these provided students with distinct opportunities to use different types of assessment, there was a lack of opportunity for students to exploit the authenticity, creativity, and wider options that multimodality can bring (Rowsell, 2013).

Within our teacher training programme (PGDE), students develop "teachers' standards" professional skills through placements in schools and working with school mentors, and these are crucial in order to graduate as a qualified teacher (Department for Education, 2019; Department for Education, 2011). The PebblePad platform provided us the opportunity for a major overhaul and modernisation of this whole process as well as providing students with an enhanced digital experience which aligns to the University's strategic vision (PebblePad, ndB).

The Problem

Our case study demonstrates the versatility of PebblePad by describing how we use PebblePad in two distinct ways:

- In academic programmes as an alternative to the essay, leveraging alternative sources, creativity, and multimedia;
- In vocational settings as a powerful professional development tool.

A key educational driver across the University of Sheffield is to enhance the student experience through active learning environments which empower the students to take control of their learning and build up their own knowledge and skills (Opre, et al., 2022.). We aim to achieve this through the use of a range of digital tools for both learning and assessment, streamlining the traditional offline methods previously used.

Academic programmes

Across several academic programmes there was a growing need within assessment to enable students to utilise a range of non-academic sources and present them within their work in a variety of ways, such as embedding videos, audio, images, and other media. We were looking for ways that students could create online multimedia "portfolios" (or websites) that would also fit into our existing assessment management workflow in Blackboard. When looking for potential tools, PebblePad offered us both a multimedia authoring tool and a strong integration with our existing assessment management workflow.

Vocational settings

A large part of our teacher training programme is based around students developing their professional skills within schools and this is supported through a professional development portfolio that combines activity logs, reflections, and assessment and feedback from school-based mentors. Pre-PebblePad, the portfolio was a 50-page word document that students completed and shared with tutors and school mentors for assessment and feedback in various ways, including printing and emailing. The whole process was antiquated, overly complex, and the antithesis of a good student experience.

When approached by the teacher training team the issues identified as needing to be addressed were:

- Terrible student experience
- No easy access for tutors and externals
- No easy process for return of feedback
- No way to monitor student progress
- Clumsy process of submission

The student experience was a priority, and having listened to the Student Voice it was clear that action needed to be taken to improve and streamline the assessment and feedback processes.

The Approach

Working with module leaders on our academic programmes to design an alternative to essays, we decided to use structured PebblePad Workbooks rather than freeform Portfolios. It was considered to be more equitable and inclusive to provide students with a limited but structured framework that they could add themed pages into, rather than the more open Portfolio structure. We felt that the more digitally literate students might be at an advantage while less adept students might struggle with the technology and be at a disadvantage. The University of Sheffield has a clear "Digital Education: Core Essentials" framework which aims to ensure that the way we teach and assess is inclusive of all students and that we do not assume that all students are digitally literate (University of Sheffield, 2023a). Our approach was to keep it simple and structured so that students could focus on the content and not have to worry about learning PebblePad.

We created PebblePad Workbooks for three modules. These workbooks break down the essay format into themed sections that work together. Each workbook is like a roadmap, providing dedicated pages for different parts of the essay. For example, the workbook for the 1st year BA module "Social and Historical Constructions of Childhood" is broken down into pages for introduction, methodology, investigation, conclusion, and references. This offers a more relaxed learning environment where students can explore, discuss, and reflect on both academic and non-academic sources. This helps them develop their academic skills in a less formal setting before tackling more structured essay writing..

Initially the decision was made to use the auto-submit function within PebblePad. However, feedback from students indicated that this caused confusion, despite the process being explained. The auto-submit led to students raising help requests with the departmental and central teams, panicking that they had submitted a final version. To make their experience more consistent with other assessment practices, we made the decision to allow students to manually submit when they felt ready to share their work. While this removes the element of progress tracking by tutors it was decided that for summative assessments like these, it would not be an issue and the student experience took priority.

In our teacher training programme, it was clear that the professional development component was in need of an overhaul and after researching various platforms, we decided to use PebblePad for the following reasons:

- Ability to build and distribute a Workbook
- Ability to build Workbook pages with a variety of fields/forms
- Automatic submission and synchronous tutor view of students' work
- Ability to share with external assessors
- Tutors and externals can leave feedback in a variety of ways
- Assessor-only fields
- Students can instantly access new feedback

The first task was to unpick the old 50-page paper-based portfolio and see how parts of this might translate to PebblePad. This was a time-consuming process, however it encouraged the teaching team to review the whole assessment, in light of the new technology, and make significant changes and enhancements.

The result was a multi-page Workbook combining a range of PebblePad block types that closely aligned with the activities students are required to do and the ways in which they need to be documented. This includes tables where students can log activities with dates, text blocks for structured reflections, and assessor-only areas using text and binary blocks.

As this is a continuous formative assessment process, we decided that these Workbooks should auto-submit. We found that this made sense to students as they see their development portfolio as very different to other assessments given that it spans the whole course and provides tutors and externals with continuous access to their work.

One key feature of PebblePad is the ability to add external assessors. This is vital to our teacher training programme as students spend the majority of their time in schools developing their skills alongside their school mentors. The ability to grant mentors access to their students' portfolios as assessors means that mentors have a continuous focal point where they can monitor, provide feedback, and assess their students' progress.

The external assessor functionality in PebblePad also saved the department significant admin time previously required to register computer accounts centrally to provide access to digital tools. The bulk creation tool within PebblePad enabled the easy adding of ~350 externals to the workspace. This was later reviewed and now the students have the responsibility to add their own external assessor to share work with them. Whilst some additional training was needed, it is a much easier process to allow external markers to mark in PebblePad than other university systems.

The whole process of getting the assessments to where they are today has taken 5 years, with reviews to identify improvements after each intake completes their studies. These improvements were then changed in the next iteration of the Workbook for the next cohort, avoiding any possible data loss that can be caused when editing a live Workbook.

The Results

We have now successfully embedded PebblePad across multiple programmes within the School of Education. We have developed a range of PebblePad Workbooks that have been adapted to suit the needs of particular modules and programmes and we continue to improve on these.

Integrating PebblePad has been challenging at times and we have developed and adapted how we manage PebblePad assessments to better align with our internal processes. There has been much discussion and debate around PebblePad, however the minutes from a recent School Education Committee state that "It was agreed that PebblePad had improved and has both creative and functional benefits".

An additional outcome from the use of PebblePad in teacher training is the adoption and roll-out of a similar workflow in the Doctor of Educational Psychology (DEdPsy) programme, to support the professional competency development that constitutes the basis for The Health and Care Professions Council (HCPC) professional qualification. This PebblePad Workbook spans the three-year programme and maps over 100 individual competencies via capability blocks. This replaces a paper-based process and gives the students the ability to self-assess and evidence their progression through each competency. It provides external "Workplace Supervisors" access to give feedback and approve their students' progress, and University tutors can also monitor progression. This also provides students with a comprehensive record of their activities, experiences, skills, competencies, and collected evidence that they can use in other assessments and take away at the end of their course.

Lessons Learnt

For students, using PebblePad for assessment is very different to just submitting an assay or other file. We learned that it was important to provide students with lots of specific information about how to start their Workbook, how to create pages for the Workbook, working with different media, and crucially how to submit their work. This was done through screencasts and face-to-face demonstrations.

In early iterations, we used the automatic submission method for summative assessment. This caused much confusion for some students as it is a fairly abstract concept that is not consistent with usual ways of submitting an assignment at the end of a module. So, for summative assessments we now always require students to manually submit and for our formative professional development portfolios that span the whole course, we use auto-submit.

While ATLAS provides a good integration with Blackboard, there have been issues with integration into our normal assessment workflows. Some of this has been technical, but often this has been where admin staff are unfamiliar with the tools, have a lack of understanding or where we have to create exceptions within the normal process. Two key examples for this have been in providing extensions and in the release of marks and feedback. The issue with these has not been a lack of but too much functionality. Through focussed documentation and working one-to-one, colleagues now have a better understanding of how ATLAS works and are comfortable with any variations in workflows needed to accommodate PebblePad.

Anonymous marking is an important part of assessment for Quality Assurance purposes and we were able to do this in PebblePad through setting permissions so markers could not see author details. However, this caused unforeseen problems later in the assessment process when trying to identify which submissions to include in moderation samples (we use a separate Set for this in ATLAS). Anonymous submissions are identified with a code rather than a student name, but we found that each code was unique to each staff member, so there was no way for a team of markers to identify specific students or submissions to be included in a moderation sample set. We devised a workaround where anonymisation would be turned off temporarily while a sample was collated, then turned on again for moderation.

While the two professional development trackers (PGDE and DEdCPsy) clearly provide students with an invaluable resource, tutors have noted a few areas where they would like to see improvements:

- In the DEdCPsy competency tracker – the ability to see progress for a student across all Capabilities in an ATLAS report, rather than a single Workbook page.
- In the PGDE teacher development portfolio – the ability to make tables available as assessor-only fields would vastly improve the external assessor wrokflow.

In Brief

- PebblePad enabled the development of the assessment process in the School of Education and allowed for a more streamlined process and student experience.
- The use of PebblePad has been adopted in other programmes within the school after the success of the initial PGDE Workbook
- Auto-submit is used selectively - whilst it makes sense to those of us who use the system on a daily basis, students found it too different from the processes they are used to.
- Our implementation was not problem free, and we had to adapt processes as we went along, e.g. anonymous marking issues.

Feedback

"As a student with a SpLD, using the PebblePad Workbook really helped to break down the work into manageable chunks and being able to use non-academic sources helped me to express my thoughts."

L1 BA student.

"The in–built reflection opportunity using PebblePad enhanced the learning further by giving cause and time to ponder about the process from different angles."

MA DLCE student (digital portfolio)

"Everyone who needs to can see it. Great for sharing progress across the two placements. Students can use it quite flexibly within the structure. You can do "reports", so it's easy to moderate a particular section (provided it's not in a table!!!). We used this, for example, to moderate the targets that school-based mentors were setting, which led to a bit of work on doing this effectively."

PGDE Tutor

"It is a useful interface between PGDE tutors and school mentors."

PGDE Tutor

"[We] find it useful as a creative tool for [our] programmes"

PGT and PGR programme directors

"It can cause panic for BA Level 1 students for their first assessment, but then students at BA open days often cite that they enjoy the creative freedom that PebblePad allows."

BA Lecturer

References

Department for Education. (2011). *Teachers' standards: Overview*. UK Government Department for Education. https://assets.publishing.service.gov.uk/media/5a750668ed915d3c7d529cad/Teachers_standard_information.pdf

Department for Education. (2019). *Initial teacher training (ITT): core content framework* (Department for Education publication DFE-00015-2019). UK Government Department for Education. https://assets.publishing.service.gov.uk/media/6061eb9cd3bf7f5cde260984/ITT_core_content_framework_.pdf

Opre, D., Șerban, C., Veșcan, A., & Iucu, R. (2022). Supporting students' active learning with a computer based tool. *Active Learning in Higher Education*. https://doi.org/10.1177/14697874221100465

PebblePad. (ndA). ePortfolio Features and Functionality Checklist [Brochure]. https://pebblepad.com/resources/guide/eportfolio-features-functionality-checklist/

PebblePad [ndB]. Empowering students to become career-ready at Edge Hill University [Case Study]. https://pebblepad.com/resources/case-study/empowering-students-career-ready-edge-hill-university/

Roswell, J. (2013). Working with multimodality: Rethinking Literacy in a Digital Age. Taylor & Francis. https://ebookcentral.proquest.com/lib/sheffield/detail.action?docID=1104812.

University of Sheffield. (2023a). Digital Education: Core Essentials. https://staff.sheffield.ac.uk/digital-learning-tools/core-essentials [Note: Behind staff log in]

University of Sheffield. (2023b). Priority three: Digital Experience. https://www.sheffield.ac.uk/vision/our-pillars/education/digital-experience

4

Casting the net wide: The "conflict of efficiencies" and large scale PebblePad workflows at the University of Edinburgh.

Robert Chmielewski
Information Services, University of Edinburgh, UK

Introduction

As per the title of this paper, I am referencing the "casting the net wide" idiom. Generally, the phrase describes a fishing net which is spread wide enough so that it captures all types of "catches", and therefore ensures the inclusion of the most desired "catch".

Having been involved in designing and supporting the PebblePad implementations at our University for 16 years, I often picture the PebblePad/ATLAS system as a flexible "net" - especially given the system's flexible range of functionalities. As part of my professional practice, this "net" is then spread in such a way that we are able to catch all of the aspects of the challenging requirements of a given assessment workflow.

However, the question of whether and/or how the "net" (PebblePad) is technically capable of ensuring required coverage is not the issue I will be discussing here. The focus of my analysis is not how to deploy PebblePad at scale to ensure that it can simply support a particular workflow. Instead, I will be attempting to capture my observations around the act of casting the "net" from the efficiency point of view of its main groups of users. Moreover, I am reflecting on the varied costs of "casting the net wide" when confronted with the requirements of "large scale" and "efficiency".

The Context and the Approach

Whilst relying on varying workflows, PebblePad is used across the University of Edinburgh (UoE) for a number of educational activities at a course, programme and cross institutional levels. These include reflective blogging, vocational portfolios, reflective portfolios, experiential learning frameworks, multiple marking, etc.

For someone who supports PebblePad as one of our University's centrally available services, I am usually involved in all of the stages of most initiatives which are exploring the system with the intention of implementing it. As outlined above, some of our use cases can be seen as matching the system's headline workflows very well. These include activities such as simple blogging, basic Workbook submissions, and personal portfolios which often follow the generally uncomplicated and relatively intuitive user experience pathways.

However, there are other practices which we are able to host in PebblePad where the system acts as a platform upon which we develop more complex workflows - to be rolled out to large groups of students.

These include, amongst others, the three case studies analysed in this paper:

1. Multilevel Workbooks which host PebblePocket-generated evidence.
2. Mass peer-review exercises for 1000s of feedback responses.
3. The "double-blind" marking of dissertations managed simultaneously over two ATLAS workspaces.

Back in 2017-2020, when we were exploring PebblePad as the host system for these workflows, we departed from viewing PebblePad as "an e-portfolio", "not just an eportfolio" or even "the personal learning space". PebblePad was thought of as a very flexible environment that offers a rich collection of built-in "assessment processing" tools which can be creatively used to automate/streamline some of the time-consuming processes.

Nonetheless, by attempting to rely on PebblePad in ways which depart from its headline utility, we introduced extra complexity on the instructional, as well as the practical, levels. As these less standard configurations were put in place, all of the three main groups of PebblePad users (admins, students and markers) risked being exposed to a proportionately more complex range of instructional prompts and system tasks. This could mean that the overall setup would suffer from poor user experience, become difficult to manage, and deemed inefficient. In order to prevent this, considerable effort was dedicated to ensuring that such risks were reduced, or at least remained well balanced. It resulted in an interesting disharmony - given the fact that the demands of each of the groups of users appeared to be dissonant from one another.

The following is an introduction to the three case studies which I will be using as examples when later exploring the nature of this friction in more depth.

Example 1: Gathering and examining medical students' evidence of learning using complex Workbooks (based at the UoE's School of Medicine).

In this example Workbooks are embedded as sections within the yearly master Workbooks. The initiative involves well over 1,000 ongoing Workbook submissions annually with each Workbook designed to accommodate dozens of pages of PebblePocket-generated evidence. The Workbooks also accommodate Assessor Fields, evidence "sign off" elements, and much more.

Example 2: Large scale peer-marking of student exchange applications (based at UoE's Edinburgh Global).

This example includes around 6000 student peer reviews attached annually to a thousand exchange applications, with students using Pebble⁺ templates for submissions, and later acting as markers in ATLAS using Feedback Templates.

Example 3: Dissertation marking to accommodate the double-blind marking workflow (based at the three UoE's Schools - Business, Divinity and Law).

This workflow involves ATLAS being used as a vehicle for two-stage marking across two separate workspaces, each utilising many tools such as Approvals, Feedback templates, and Turnitin via ATLAS, and involving multiple markers per submission.

As already mentioned, what unites these three case studies is their sheer scale as well their high level of customisation and complexity, i.e. spanning multiple workspaces, utilising the desktop and mobile versions, allowing multiple assessments from various markers, and dealing with very high numbers of submissions. All of these custom workflows were developed in response to very specific, and often substantial, lists of requirements. Given the intricacies which such setups naturally exhibit, they were perceived as potentially prone to generating large amounts of friction for their users (students, markers and admins). Therefore, during the design stage meetings, special attention needed to be paid to the issue of overall efficiency around the user interactions with the system and its elements.

In all of the examples, these setups had to appear: very accessible yet with multiple points of access; simple to operate yet powerful; uncluttered and at the same time able to offer a wide range of options; and so on. Despite the juxtapositional nature of these ambitious projects, we continued to develop ways of counterbalancing the rich nature of the original sets of requirements. In other words, whilst the demands which were put on PebblePad were heavy, the effort required to use the system had be made as light as possible.

In order to explore the nature of this pursuit for the purpose of preparing this paper, I looked back at my notes from the meetings, discussions and feedback sessions from the time we were working on the three case studies. Focusing on the tensions outlined above, I attempted to systemise them and/or break them down further. This in turn allowed me to propose the following four distinctive perspectives (listed below), outlining the key strategies to achieve "efficiency" for each use case. They consist of responses that were produced based on the different target groups and their different views of what would make the system more efficient for them.

Table 1: Perspective 1 - System efficiency from the system point of view

The system	Example 1: Complex Workbooks	Example 2: Large scale peer marking	Example 3: Double-blind marking of dissertations
Ensure that unique and complex requirements match with PebblePad's functionalities	Multilevel Workbooks Flexible management of submissions Seamless integration with the mobile app	Flexible management of ~1000 template-based submissions during a week-long exercise Distribution of ~6000 reviews	Flexible management of dynamically changing permissions for multiple markers Bespoke feedback templates

The system	Example 1: Complex Workbooks	Example 2: Large scale peer marking	Example 3: Double-blind marking of dissertations
Ensure high accessibility and high level of reliability of the system	Interface always present in the desktop browser tab (no pop-ups) Simple mobile interface	Reduced number of ATLAS buttons Compatibility with tablets and mobiles	Reduced number of ATLAS buttons Seamlessly embedded integration with Turnitin
Maximise the proportion of bespoke elements of the interface	Bespoke banners Bespoke instructions for markers	Role and Sets-based permissions to maximise customisation	Visual indicators of rates of completion across the stages of the workflow
Adjust the structure of submissions to match the locally preferred patterns	Yearly Workbooks where evidence is split into sub-Workbooks	Simple submission templates with numeric/grading feedback templates	Duality of types of feedback (including hidden feedback)

Table 2: Perspective 2 - System efficiency from the student point of view

The students	Example 1: Complex Workbooks	Example 2: Large scale peer marking	Example 3: Double-blind marking of dissertations
Reduce potential technical difficulties	Highlight the difference between the desktop account vs PebblePocket app	Provide very specific instructions alongside specific dates for completion	Bypass Pebble+ and present ATLAS as the main interface
Minimise the complexity of the system's access route	Provide direct links to Workbooks and assignment upload pages in ATLAS	Generate direct links and share them for each stage of the exercise	Generate direct links and share them for each stage of the exercise
Minimise friction when working on submissions	Automate the Workbook submission process	Send the students automatically to the template's original copy (before the deadline)	Support file submission replacements up until the deadline

Table 3: Perspective 3 - System efficiency from the marker point of view

The markers	Example 1: Complex Workbooks	Example 2: Large scale peer marking	Example 3: Double-blind marking of dissertations
Maximise the visibility of the marking material	Provide direct links to assignments/ workspaces Use Sets in ATLAS	Rely on custom Sets in ATLAS Generate direct links to the workspace	Rely on custom Sets in ATLAS Generate direct links to the workspace
Maximise the proportion of bespoke feedback templates	Insert Assessor Fields into the Workbook sections Use the offline 'sign off' in PebblePocket	Keep feedback templates heavily structured with no open question input	Offer detailed feedback templates Embed bespoke instructions for Approvals in the interface

Table 4: Perspective 4 - System efficiency from the admin point of view

The admins	Example 1: Complex Workbooks	Example 2: Large scale peer marking	Example 3: Double-blind marking of dissertations
Simplify the management of a particular setup – in isolation to the whole system	Rely on duplication of golden copies when creating new instances of workspaces Adjust the permissions at Region level in ATLAS	Rely on duplication of golden copies when creating new instances of workspaces	Rely on duplication of golden copies when creating new instances of workspaces
Simplify ways of checking the correctness of the setup	Develop settings checklists/notes to be shared internally	Develop settings checklists/notes to be shared internally	Develop settings checklists/notes to be shared internally

The admins	Example 1: Complex Workbooks	Example 2: Large scale peer marking	Example 3: Double-blind marking of dissertations
Maximise the amount of bespoke indicators for continuous monitoring	Generate reports for released and unreleased Assessor Fields Monitor Logs in ATLAS Utilise the past version snapshots in ATLAS	Generate reports on "Submission status" Monitor Logs in ATLAS Utilise past version snapshots in ATLAS	Offer visualisation of the three-level Approvals Monitor Feedback Templates reports to eliminate minor feedback absences

The Results

Naturally, the above list of actions/interventions is not exhaustive but merely a sample selected to illustrate the issue. Interestingly, upon closer inspection, it is not difficult to determine the tensions between the directions in which some of these interventions seem to be pulling. For instance, in Example 1, the Workbooks are embedded within Workbooks and include assessor fields as well as the multiple evidence placeholders to increase their overall efficiency for the students, i.e. all of the artefacts are in one collection (Workbook). At the same time, the drive for the administrative efficiency pushes towards more easily duplicated setups as well as more accessible reporting mechanisms (which become more difficult to deliver the more complex these Workbooks become). Similarly, in Example 2, the efforts to simplify the interface to benefit the students can be seen as in contrast to the push by the administrators to be able to manage and control the submissions and the feedback flexibly. Furthermore, as seen in Example 3, the need for regular monitoring of the double-workspace setup can be deemed time inefficient by the admins. However, this requirement is generated by the flexible marking deadlines, which allow the markers to go about their task more efficiently.

These observations point to the challenge which the designers of these workflows (and consequently the designers of the PebblePad/ATLAS platform) face when trying to harmonise the drive towards increased efficiency across the main user groups. Reflecting on the above examples, I identify at least four main "conflicts" which I believe are worth highlighting here:

- Portability of multilevel submissions vs ease of monitoring them at the admin level.
- Students' ease of access vs less laborious workspace management.
- Uncluttered interface vs enhanced system management options.
- Greater flexibility for markers vs reduced amount of manual admin interventions.

The ways forward

On top of the simple interventions outlined above, I revisited ideas around potential future changes which could make positive impact on the issues highlighted. As a result of discussions with colleagues who are locally involved in supporting the three workflows, we developed a range of feedback as well as feature requests which could improve the experiences of each of the main groups of users.

Table 5: Summary of feedback and feature requests to improve complex workflows

Type of feedback	Example 1: Complex Workbooks	Example 2: Large scale peer marking	Example 3: Double-blind marking of dissertations
Highlight any functionalities which are missing	Dynamic monitoring of missing/ completed sections of the Workbook Selective signalling of sections in need of marking	Automated distribution of students across peer marking groups	Automated shifting of partially marked dissertations between the two main workspaces
Reflect on mismatched expectations vs. actual system behaviour	Overall setup seen as labour intensive by local support staff	Overall setup perceived as overwhelming by newly appointed local support staff	Two-workspace setup requiring constant monitoring Turnitin anonymity inflexibility vs ATLAS assignment settings
Question the balance of effort between the main groups of users	Large accessible Workbooks seem portable for Students, but harder to penetrate en masse for Admins	Potential minor admin errors can be majorly impacting 1000s of submissions within days Students expected to be familiar with the Marker view	Labour intensive process of managing individual Sets Room for human error when calculating the final grade

The above observations seem to be suggesting at least two main ways forward:

- The various feature requests suggest a focus on enhancing elements which already form the current users' journeys - more in-depth reporting for admins; automated distribution of students; built-in automation for grade calculations for markers, etc.
- The user perceptions of the system suggest a vision of PebblePad where the system presents itself in the most suitable 'disguise' depending on the role of the user accessing it. One could argue that this vision has already been achieved to an extent, with PebblePad already split into Pebble+ and ATLAS. However, in many cases (including the above examples) the actual users' pathways still cut through both of these main areas exposing them to potentially less relevant functionalities.

Conclusion

PebblePad can act as a versatile and efficient vehicle for a number of the large scale and complex higher educational assessment workflows. On one hand this efficiency means that the scale of the system's operational complexity expands in proportion with the complexity of the original requirements. On the other hand, the weight of the tasks means that the users require a different type of efficiency by allowing them to interact with the system in ways which are simple and intuitive. Such a dichotomy creates the "conflict of efficiencies" which can affect most of the complex and large scale PebblePad implementations. This presents an interesting user experience challenge which can be partially overcome by attempting to satisfy some of the feature enhancements highlighted in this paper. The topic deserves further investigation - hopefully resulting in new and creative ways of harmonising these differing perceptions of PebblePad's efficiency.

5

Enhancing professional identity and capability in a transdisciplinary programme through ongoing reflection using PebblePad.

Buena Jill Galleposo, Susanne Lorenz, Cathy Malone, & Harriet Thew
School of Earth and Environment, University of Leeds, UK

Introduction

The climate crisis is one of the most pressing and complex challenges of our time, requiring urgent and coordinated action from multiple stakeholders across different sectors and disciplines. However, the traditional disciplinary boundaries and silos that dominate the academic and professional landscape often hinder the development and implementation of effective and innovative solutions (Adefila, et al., 2021). Transdisciplinary approaches, which aim to integrate knowledge, methods, and perspectives from different disciplines and sectors to collaboratively address a common problem, have been proposed as a promising way to tackle the climate crisis and its multifaceted impacts (Yeung, et al., 2021). Such approaches enable experts from various relevant fields to cooperate and access different viewpoints and novel ideas that single disciplines may overlook (Boger, et al., 2017). Therefore, for complex real-world problems like the climate crisis, the quality and effectiveness of the solutions depend on the level of collaboration, communication, and integration among the team members, which can be achieved with transdisciplinarity.

However, transdisciplinary collaboration poses many challenges, such as communication barriers, power dynamics, and conflicting values and interests amongst participants (Brazadauskaite & Rasimaviciene, 2015; Dannecker, 2020). It is essential to equip the current and future generations of climate professionals with skills, competencies, and mindsets that enable them to work effectively, efficiently, and equitably in transdisciplinary, international teams.

The Context

In this case study, we present a new transdisciplinary postgraduate programme, MSc Climate Futures, which draws upon a range of disciplines to address the complexity of the climate crisis. The programme is designed to develop students' professional identities and enhance their capabilities, empowering them to make substantive contributions to meaningful climate action. Recognising the imperative for individuals with multifaceted skills and perspectives, the emphasis on developing professional identity and capability within the transdisciplinary framework ensures graduates are well-equipped to navigate the complexities of the climate crisis and actively participate in transformative initiatives (Hancock & Walsh, 2016; Monereo, 2022; Yeung, et al., 2021).

Intended Learning Outcomes

Our transdisciplinary master's programme recognises that to effectively engage with multifaceted and complex challenges posed by the climate crisis, students must develop a strong professional identity and capability, which involves not only the acquisition of knowledge but also the development of affective and behavioural skills such as empathy, curiosity, creativity, resilience, and ethical awareness (Thew, et al., 2021).

The importance of these skills lies in their ability to facilitate effective engagement with the diverse aspects of climate-related issues. For instance, empathy allows students to understand the perspectives of different stakeholders (Hallin, et al., 2018), while creativity and resilience enable them to devise and implement innovative solutions even in the face of setbacks (Moleka, 2023). However, the transdisciplinary nature of this programme presents a significant challenge: the need for effective communication and collaboration across disciplinary boundaries and within multidisciplinary, international teams (Brazdauskaite & Rasimaviciene, 2015). This necessitates not only cognitive and technical skills but also the cultivation of interpersonal and intercultural competencies, such as communication, listening, respect, and trust. These skills are not just supplementary; they are fundamental to fostering effective collaboration and integrating diverse perspectives into climate solutions (Thew, et al., 2021). By enhancing these skills, we are not only equipping students to tackle the climate crisis but also strengthening their professional identity, preparing them to become effective and resilient climate change professionals. This underscores the importance of developing a strong professional identity within the programme.

The programme also aims to encourage students to engage in ongoing reflection on their skills and aspirations. This reflective practice enables students to align their learning journeys with key competencies such as self-awareness, normative competency, and anticipatory thinking (Sankar & Tripathy, 2014), as recommended by Rieckmann (2017) for Education for Sustainable Development. By fostering these competencies, the programme does more than just equip students with knowledge and skills. It empowers them to navigate the complexities of the climate crisis and contribute meaningfully to sustainable development efforts. In doing so, it enhances their professional identity and capability, preparing them to be effective change agents in their respective fields. Thus, ongoing reflection serves as a powerful tool in this programme to bridge the gap between academic learning and professional practice, ultimately contributing to the development of well-rounded professionals.

Finally, the programme aims to alleviate eco-anxiety by empowering learners to challenge their assumptions and carve out their own pathways to impact. By supporting students in this way, the programme not only equips them with the skills and knowledge to tackle the climate crisis but also enhances their professional identity, thereby preparing them to be effective and resilient climate change professionals (Cruickshank & Fenner, 2012; Howlett, et al., 2016).

The Approach

Our transdisciplinary master's programme aims to prepare students for the complex and urgent challenges of the climate crisis by developing their interdisciplinary competencies, skills, and knowledge. However, this also involves several pedagogical and practical difficulties, such as fostering reflection and self-awareness, developing professional identities and capabilities, facilitating evidence gathering and analysis, and managing eco-anxiety. To address these difficulties, we are utilising PebblePad, a digital portfolio platform, as a key strategy to enhance the learning outcomes and experiences of our students. We argue that PebblePad offers a comprehensive, dynamic, collaborative, flexible, and robust solution for transdisciplinary learning.

PebblePad, as a tool for ongoing reflection, plays a pivotal role in helping our programme address the challenges that a transdisciplinary programme face. For instance, we are using PebblePad to enable students to engage meaningfully with various facets of climate-related challenges. As PebblePad supports reflective activities and integrative learning, students can create, store, and share diverse forms of evidence of their learning experiences, such as assignments, reflections, feedback, artifacts, and achievements (Campbell, 2019). By using PebblePad, students can document and showcase their learning journey in a comprehensive and meaningful way and demonstrate their achievement of the intended learning outcomes of the programme. Moreover, PebblePad enables students to reflect on their strengths and areas for improvement, and to receive feedback and recognition for their work from various audiences, such as peers, mentors, employers, and the wider public. This process fosters self-awareness, self-regulation, and self-efficacy, which are essential for developing a professional identity and capability in the context of the climate crisis (Howlett, et al., 2016). PebblePad also facilitates the development of other key skills, such as empathy, curiosity, creativity, and resilience, by providing a platform for students to explore diverse perspectives, generate innovative solutions, learn from setbacks, and adapt to changing challenges and opportunities. Therefore, PebblePad, as a tool for ongoing reflection, plays an important role in honing the necessary skills to face climate-related challenges.

The transdisciplinary nature of our program requires effective communication and collaboration across disciplinary boundaries and within multidisciplinary, international teams. This is a complex and challenging task, as it involves integrating diverse perspectives, knowledge, and methods into climate solutions (Thew, et al., 2021). PebblePad supports this task by encouraging reflection on interpersonal and intercultural competencies, such as communication, listening, respect, and trust. These competencies are not mere supplements but foundational to collaboration and knowledge co-production, as they enable mutual understanding, learning, and negotiation among collaborators (Hallin, et al., 2018). Furthermore, PebblePad facilitates the exchange of insights and knowledge among students and mentors, as well as with external stakeholders and communities, enhancing the quality and diversity of the learning outcomes. PebblePad also allows students to showcase their work and impact to various audiences and receive feedback and recognition for their work (Campbell, 2019). Therefore, PebblePad becomes an instrumental tool for addressing the transdisciplinary challenge of our program.

Lastly, PebblePad serves as a vital tool for alleviating our students' eco-anxiety by empowering learners to reflect on their assumptions, cultivate critical thinking, and proactively carve out unique pathways to impact (Eriksson, et al., 2022). The platform's affordance for reflection supports students in documenting coping strategies and fostering resilience, thereby addressing the emotional challenges associated with engaging with the climate crisis (Pihkala, 2021). By encouraging ongoing reflection, PebblePad not only contributes to a nuanced understanding of environmental challenges but also shapes students' professional identity as effective climate change professionals.

By using PebblePad, our students can develop their interdisciplinary competencies, skills, and knowledge, as well as their professional identities and capabilities, through ongoing reflection, evidence gathering, and feedback. PebblePad also enables our students to collaborate across disciplines and cultures, and to communicate and share their work with various audiences and stakeholders. Moreover, PebblePad empowers our students to cope with their eco-anxiety and to take action and contribute to climate solutions. Therefore, we believe that PebblePad is an invaluable tool for transdisciplinary learning and for preparing our students for the complex and urgent challenges of the 21st century.

Implementation

In order to support ongoing reflection for developing professional identity and capabilities within the students, we utilised PebblePad in our programme in the following ways:

1. We provided training on the concept, practice, and value of reflection at the outset of the course, as well as on how to use PebblePad, recognising that students might not be familiar with its interface and functionalities.
2. We designed a template on PebblePad to structure and scaffold their reflections throughout the course, using the 5Rs of reflection by Bain, et al. (2002), which include Reporting, Responding, Relating, Reasoning, and Reconstructing the experience. However, we also created a more unstructured PebblePad Blog to allow differentiation, acknowledging that students reflect in different ways and that it is personal to them.
3. We provided students with regular prompts to stimulate deep thinking about their academic and professional growth, which includes targeted reflections on key moments of experiential learning within and beyond the classroom, and open-ended reminders for students to document moments of significance for them.
4. We are offering feedback and recognition for their reflective work, both from peers and tutors. We also arranged one-on-one formative feedback sessions with the tutor to discuss their reflective practices and strategies for enhancement.

By using PebblePad, we aimed to enhance the learning outcomes and experiences of our students in a comprehensive, dynamic, collaborative, flexible, and robust way.

The Results

The initial iteration of this intervention is currently in progress. The outcomes of this phase are anticipated to contribute significantly to a reflective assignment upon the culmination of the programme. However, as the intervention is ongoing, the results remain forthcoming.

Lessons Learnt

While results are not yet available, two key lessons have already emerged from the use of PebblePad portfolio for student reflection: the importance of student-centred design; and the significance of providing early and comprehensive support throughout the process.

In this journey of using PebblePad, addressing the diversity of student experiences and backgrounds when it comes to reflection was crucial. Going in, we knew that due to the high international demographic of our students, we could not make any assumptions about their educational experiences, specifically when it comes to reflective practice. It was, therefore, important that we took this into account in our design. To accommodate this diversity in backgrounds, two distinct approaches were intentionally implemented. The first was a structured template for students new to reflection, guiding them through the process step by step, and offering scaffolding to gradually build reflective skills. The second was an informal learning journal for experienced and more confident reflectors, allowing free expression without rigid guidelines and encouraging deeper insights. One of the aims of this design was to allow inexperienced students to transition from the structured format to the more flexible learning journal as they gained confidence.

A second key lesson learned was the importance of facilitating technology acceptance by addressing perceived usefulness and perceived ease of use, as emphasised in the Technology Acceptance Model (TAM) (King & He, 2006). To ensure successful adoption of the PebblePad portfolio, collaboration across various university teams was necessary. The Digital Education Enhancement team provided pedagogical and technical expertise during the portfolio design phase to align it with educational goals, thereby enhancing perceived usefulness among students. Additionally, their focus on user experience considerations aimed to improve the perceived ease of use. Furthermore, the Library Skills team conducted sessions to familiarise students with the PebblePad functionality, further contributing to perceived ease of use. Academics also collaborated with the Library Skills team to guide students on the importance of reflection for academic and professional growth, and how to effectively utilise PebblePad for reflective practice. This joint effort sought to reinforce the perceived usefulness of the portfolio by highlighting the benefits of reflection and the tool's capability to support this process. Ultimately, by addressing both perceived usefulness and perceived ease of use through a coordinated, cross-functional approach, we hoped that the implementation of PebblePad would be better positioned for successful technology acceptance among students.

This experience underscores the importance of tailoring tools to student needs and providing robust support from the outset. By doing so, we believe that students are more likely to engage meaningfully with the reflective process as facilitated by PebblePad.

In Brief

- Reflection is an important skill which many postgraduate students may not have previous experience of in an educational-setting.
- Capturing reflections as part of the learning experience is valuable in supporting students to recognise their own personal and professional development.
- Student reflections provide useful insights for pedagogical evaluation and subsequent module and programme development.

References

Adefila, A., Chen, Y.F., Dang, Q., & Dewinter, A. (2021). Integrating sustainability-oriented ecologies of practice across the learning cycle: Supporting transformative behaviours in transgenerational, transnational and transdisciplinary spaces. *Discourse and Communication for Sustainable Education, 12(2)*, 142-154. https://doi.org/10.2478/dcse-2021-0022

Bain, J.D., Ballatyne, R., Mills, C., & Lester, N.C. (2002). *Reflection on practice: Student teachers' perspectives*. Post Pressed.

Boger, J., Jackson, P., Mulvenna, M., Sixsmith, J., Sixsmith, A., Mihalidis, A., Kontos, P., Polgar, J.M., Grigorovich, A., & Martin, S. (2017). Principles for fostering the transdisciplinary development of assistive technologies. *Disability and Rehabilitation, 12(5)*, 480-490. https://doi.org/10.3109/17483107.2016.1151953

Brazdauskaite, G., & Rasimaviciene, D. (2015). Towards the creative university: Developing a conceptual framework for transdisciplinary teamwork. *Journal of Creativity and Business Innovation, 1*, 49-63.

Campbell, C. (2019). Creating a successful implementation of PebblePad: The university context. In C.N. Allan, C. Campbell, & J. Crough (Eds.), *Blended Learning Designs in STEM Higher Education: Putting Learning First* (pp. 17-34). Springer.

Cruickshank, H. & Fenner, R., (2012). Exploring key sustainable development themes through learning activities. *International Journal of Sustainability in Higher Education, 13(3)*, 249-262.

Dannecker, P. (2020). Transdisciplinarity 'meets' power structures: Challenges and experiences of a capacity building project on transdisciplinarity, *Austrian Journal of South-East Asian Studies, 13(2)*, 175-192.

Eriksson, E., Peters, A. K., Pargman, D., Hedin, B., Laurell-Thorslund, M., & Sjöö, S. (2022). Addressing students' eco-anxiety when teaching sustainability in higher education. In *2022 International Conference on ICT for Sustainability (ICT4S)*, 88-98. IEEE.

Hallin, J., Mantel, N.A., & Carter, C. (2018). What purpose does a company serve in the world? Swedish students and sustainability professionals in dialogue on corporate sustainability. *Journal of Business Theory and Practice, 6(3)*, 202-210. https://doi.org/10.22158/jbtp.v6n3p202

Hancock, S., & Walsh, E. (2016). Beyond knowledge and skills: Rethinking development of professional identity during the STEM doctorate, *Studies in Higher Education, 41(1)*, 37-50. https://doi.org/10.1080/03075079.2014.915301

Howlett, C., Ferreira, J.A. & Blomfield, J. (2016). Teaching sustainable development in higher education: Building critical, reflective thinkers through an interdisciplinary approach. *International Journal of Sustainability in Higher Education, 17(3)*, 305–321.

King, W.R. & He, J. (2006). A meta-analysis of the technology acceptance model. *Information & management, 43(6)*, 740-755.

Moleka, P. (2023). Innovative leadership in addressing climate change: A pathway towards sustainable futures. *Preprints*. https://doi.org/10.20944/preprints202310.0376.v1

Monereo, C. (2022). The identity of education professionals: *Positioning, training, and innovation.* Information Age Publishing.

Pihkala, P. (2021). Eco-anxiety. In C.P. Krieg & R. Toivanen (Eds.), *Situating Sustainability: A Handbook of Contexts and Concepts* (pp. 119-133). Helsinki University Press. https://doi.org/10.33134/HUP-14-9

Rieckmann, M. (2017). *Education for sustainable development goals: Learning objectives.* UNESCO publishing.

Sankar, S., & Tripathy, L.K. (2014). Changing dynamics in the role of management education & faculty competencies for sustainable development. *Proceedings of Emerging Trends & Practices in Indian Business Environment*, 85-91.

Thew, H., Graves, C., Reay, D., Smith, S., Petersen, K., Bomberg, E., Boxley, S., Causley, J., Congreve, A., Cross, I., Dunk, R., Dunlop, L., Facer, K., Gamage, K. A. A., Greenhalgh, C., Greig, A., Kiamba, L., Kinakh, V., Kioupi, V., Lee, M., Klapper, R., Kurul, E., Marshall-Cook, J., McGivern, A., Mörk, J., Nijman, V., O'Brien, J., Preist, C., Price, E., Samangooei, M., Schrodt, F., Sharmina, M., Toney, J., Walsh, C., Walsh, T., Wood, R. Wood, P., and Worsfold, N.T. (2021). Mainstreaming climate education in Higher Education Institutions. *COP26 Universities Network Working Paper*.

Yeung, E., Carlin, L., Sandassie, S., & Jaglal, S. (2021). Transdisciplinary training: What does it take to address today's "wicked problems"?. *Innovation and Education, 3(1)*, 1-8. https://doi.org/https://doi.org/10.1186/s42862-021-00011-1

6

More than IT support: The role of the PebblePad Coordinator

Sheridan Gardiner-Klose[1] & Dr Jennifer Masters[2]
[1]Clinical Health Sciences, Nursing & Midwifery, University of South Australia, AU
[2]PebblePad, AU

The Context

The University of South Australia (UniSA) has seven Academic Units, one of which is UniSA Clinical Health and Sciences (CHS). The CHS consists of five programs, including the Nursing and Midwifery programs. In addition to postgraduate degrees, Nursing and Midwifery offers two 3-year undergraduate degrees, a Bachelor of Nursing and a Bachelor of Midwifery. These can be studied on-campus at three locations across metropolitan and regional campuses, or externally (mostly online), with some on campus workshops and industry placements. The Bachelor of Nursing is the larger of the two programs, with an intake of 851 students in 2023. The Bachelor of Midwifery has a smaller intake with 101 students commencing in 2023 year.

PebblePad was introduced in 2020 for use by all students in nursing and midwifery for clinical placements. The courses associated with clinical placements are called Experiential Learning Activities (ELAs). In Nursing, there are two 4-week focused placements and two 8-week generic placements (see Figure 1).

Figure 1: ELAs associated with clinical placement in the Bachelor of Nursing

Midwifery has 5 block clinical placements. ELAs 1, 2 & 3 are 4-week (160 hours) focused placements, while ELAs 4 and 5 are 8-week (320 hours) generic placements (see Figure 2).

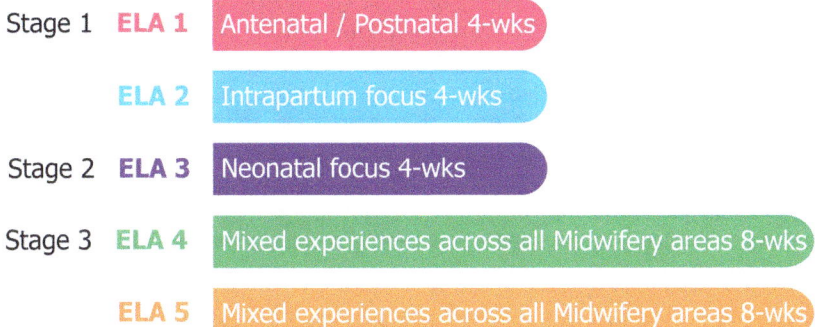

Figure 2: ELAs associated with clinical placement in the Bachelor of Midwifery

The Problem

It was clear that the paper-based system used for tracking clinical placement had too many disadvantages. Over the 3-year course students (and especially those in midwifery) could accumulate boxes of paperwork that needed to be carted in for assessment. Further, the hands-on nature of the experience led to some students handing in damaged and even smelly documentation with bits missing, as evidence of completion. This was particularly problematic if the forms held signatures for verification of competencies completed.

The Program Directors wanted an innovative, up to date, easy to use system for both staff, students, and clinical facilitators. PebblePad was identified as a possible solution, and a trial was set up with a small cohort of Nursing and Midwifery students. Only a handful of people had a basic understanding of how PebblePad worked though, and it wasn't long before the Program Directors realised that they could not do this without assistance and that it wasn't appropriate to give the course coordinators the extra workload of introducing PebblePad to staff, students, and facilitators. They took the advice of PebblePad and appointed a full time PebblePad Coordinator in March 2020 and then COVID hit.

The PebblePad Coordinator role was a brand-new position with a platform that most staff, students and clinical sites had not used before – it was a steep learning curve for all! The COVID pandemic and associated lockdowns added further complications. Basic Workbooks had been created prior to roll-out, but there were last minute changes, as student placements were cancelled, and substitute activities were quickly added to the Workbooks so that learning and assessment could continue.

The Approach

The PebblePad Coordinator role has developed over the last four years and now incorporates:

- Design and building of resources.
- Support for course coordinators, academic liaison, clinical facilitators, and students.
- Trouble shooting and building training materials.
- Enabling new uses for PebblePad.

The initial basic Workbooks provided the foundations for the detailed Workbooks that are used today. These workbooks have been developed progressively over the years based on feedback from staff, students, and facilitators. In nursing, each ELA is now supported with a comprehensive Workbook that includes course information, scope of practice, a pre-clinical assessment, a learning plan, an attendance record, a feedback and achievements section, and two self-assessments. The clinical facilitators complete weekly feedback and formative and summative assessment. The workflow is carefully managed through ATLAS, where Sets are used to ensure that students, course coordinators, academic liaison and clinical facilitators can use PebblePad with ease, in a safe and secure space.

The Midwifery Workbooks are different to the Nursing Workbooks. In the Midwifery ELAs Workbook, students complete a pre-clinical workshop, learning objectives, attendance record, clinical facilitator contact, daily feedback, Clinical assessment tools (different for each ELA), Standards Assessments and a reflection at the end of each placement. Midwifery also use collections and templates for compulsory elements of their placement. They use the sign & lock function for their Continuity of Care Experience (CoCE) and antenatal, postnatal, complex care, neonatal, labour, and birth Workbooks, as well as the templates in the ELA Workbooks. This is important because it means that these records are contemporaneous and verified at the point of care.

The Midwifery Portfolio Collection provides evidence to meet Australian Nursing & Midwifery Accreditation Council (ANMAC) requirements to register with the Australian Health Practitioner Regulation Agency (AHPRA). The requirements are extensive and include many antenatal episodes, postnatal episodes, and complex care episodes as well as records of Labour and birth experiences and neonatal examinations. They also need to provide 'continuity of care' (CoCE) records for 15 women. Evidence for these requirements are tracked in a series of Workbooks that include CoCE, antenatal, postnatal, complex care, neonatal, labour and birth and the Clinical Assessment Tools (CAT). In hardcopy this created mountains of paper, and now it is all stored electronically for quick access for students, clinical facilitators, and University staff in real time.

The structure of the PebblePad Workbooks/ Midwifery collections enable students to clearly identify what is required of them. The PebblePad Workbooks provide an efficient platform to monitor progress of their requirements for both the student and the facilitator. This structure also allows staff to access documentation, verify assets and capabilities, and provide feedback and summary updates effectively and quickly.

The PebblePad Coordinator role is beyond resource design and development. Prior to the go live date, a meeting takes place between PebblePad Coordinator and the Course Coordinator to assess requirements and implement any changes. PebblePad was integrated using LTI with the LMS (Moodle) in 2022 and it was a game changer. The manual creation of Workspaces and then adding of students is no longer necessary. The Workspace still needs some adjustments, with staff and venue facilitators to be added, the allocation of roles, the addition of supporting resources and the creation of Sets, if required. Then, during clinical placement, the PebblePad Coordinator works closely with the course coordinators dealing with all students, facilitators, or staff questions and/or issues regarding PebblePad.

The PebblePad Coordinator also provides training for all staff and venue facilitators. The clinical facilitators have a training day twice a year which includes a PebblePad demonstration and Q&A if needed. An introduction to PebblePad for new UniSA staff is provided as required. When a new PebblePad account is created for a facilitator (UniSA or venue), they receive a welcome email with the user guide and the PebblePad Coordinator contact details. There is also a weekly drop-in session for students and facilitators via zoom and ad-hoc support/training is provided when needed. Occasionally the PebblePad Coordinator will visit a venue if focused training is deemed necessary. The strong relationship between the PebblePad Coordinator and key stakeholders is something that was unexpected. A sense of trust has developed, and facilitators know their emails for assistance will be answered quickly and any issues or concerns will be investigated.

Building up a bank of self-help guides and how-to resources for students, staff and facilitators has been a goal for PebblePad implementation. Often a visual guide provides a better outcome than an email reply or a conversation. This is a good strategy for saving time too. As a rule of thumb, if more than three emails on a topic or issue are received then a how-to guide should be created to explain the process.

The use of PebblePad in Nursing and Midwifery at UniSA is constantly evolving. The PebblePad Coordinator is always looking for ways to use PebblePad in smarter and more robust ways. As an example, using the 'sign and lock' function for pre-clinical workshops assessment in Midwifery wasn't working well. Some students had not followed instructions properly and this caused problems, leading to tears and delays in assessment. Swapping to using assessor fields with 'save and hold' alleviated the issues. Results are released within 48 hours, giving the course coordinator time to moderate and review any students with 'not met' evaluations. In another scenario, it was found that adding external assessors to Workspaces was difficult as the casual staff were continually changing and sometimes the assessor wouldn't have access to the assessor fields due to a last-minute replacement. The shared login option was trialed to by-pass this issue, with amazing results. This mechanism will now be used for Workspaces in the future.

The Results

Over the past four years, PebblePad has evolved from being new software that all stakeholders had to navigate as a requirement of the placement process, to a natural component of the clinical placement program that staff, students and facilitators use confidently with very little issues.

The immediacy that PebblePad offers has transformed the flow of the learning experience. Course coordinators, academic liaison, and clinical facilitators have live access to the students' Workbooks and can provide instant feedback when appropriate. The security of the digital storage of student work is also beneficial. The Workspace is a safe place for Workbooks and the days of misplaced and damaged paper Workbooks are over.

Now that PebblePad is established for the placement program, new uses are being explored. PebblePocket will be implemented in the next offering to support students at placement sites where the Internet connection isn't ideal. New ideas are being tested in the Midwifery program also, where course coordinators are keen to try out PebblePad for coursework and for supporting students as they transition into the workplace.

Lessons Learnt

The PebblePad Coordinator role was new and certainly didn't come with a rule book! There have been some important lessons learnt along the way.

It is important to be gentle, but persistent when requesting participation. Some people, both students and staff, don't like changes, especially when they are transitioning from paper to online. Excuses such as 'I'm too busy to use PebblePad' or 'I'm not tech savvy' were offered as reasons to be exempt from the new system. Opting out was not an option. All students, staff and facilitators needed to get onboard.

Training is the key to engaging stakeholders in the program. Effective training can give people the confidence to try something new, it can empower them to succeed. It is important to offer plenty of training opportunities and many of the sessions involve the PebblePad Coordinator going into the workplace, rather than expecting people to attend workshops. Getting out and meeting people is an important part of the role, and is the foundation for relationship building.

Connecting with people and building trusting relationships goes hand-in-hand with raising technical competencies. People are more likely to take risks and attempt new challenges when they know that they have someone who will look after them.

In Brief

- PebblePad is an excellent platform for digitising the placements workflow in clinical health sciences, however, it is essential to carefully design the experience for all stakeholders
- PebblePad implementation needs to be responsive. Contexts, content and players change all the time, and the PebblePad Coordinator needs to navigate the way forward.
- PebblePad support is more than IT skills; it is also about relationships, trust and being there for people.
- The PebblePad Coordinator role has been pivotal for successful implementation at UniSA. Ideally, more than one person should be able to provide this support!

Feedback

Here is some feedback received on the role of the PebblePad Coordinator:

> "I had the same issue and contacted Sheridan the PebblePad guru."
>
> From a student

"With the recent employment of a full-time staff member dedicated to PebblePad, any issues were rectified in a very timely manner. Acknowledgement needs to be made to our PebblePad Coordinator who demonstrated the ability to resolve issues swiftly, liaise with users effectively and provide ongoing education to students and clinical staff."

"It has been an absolute pleasure working alongside Sheridan. It is obvious that she is committed to improving the functionality of PebblePad and can

troubleshoot any issues very quickly, communicate with University staff, students and venue staff effectively while providing ongoing support for all."

"She has obvious strengths in the design and maintenance of software to suit user needs and has quickly grasped nursing and midwifery contexts which I understand is no means an easy feat."

From academics

"Wow Sheridan, thank you for the prompt response. I agree your previous skills have helped, but I think it's more your can-do attitude and inquisitive mind to get to the bottom of things."

From the PebblePad Customer Success Manager

7

Enhancing collaboration and content sharing across multiple Higher Educational Institutes with PebblePad

Dr Louise Grisedale
Faculty of Medicine and Health Sciences, University of East Anglia, UK

The Context

As the Course Director for Independent Prescribing (IP), I am responsible for coordinating and oversee the Nursing and Midwifery Council (NMC) and Health & Care Professions Council (HCPC) validated and Regulatory & Professional Standards Body (RPSB) accredited IP programme at the University of East Anglia (UEA) and at a satellite site, Institute B, in London.

An Independent Prescriber is a healthcare professional responsible and accountable for assessing patients with undiagnosed or diagnosed conditions and making informed decisions regarding the necessary clinical management (Department of Health, 2005). This role entails the ability to independently prescribe medications within the prescribers scope of practice, alongside other professional legislation requirements (General Pharmaceutical Council, 2022, Health and Care Professions Council, 2019, Nursing and Midwifery Council, 2018). By successfully completing our programme, learners not only fulfill their professional legislative requirements, but also meet the criteria stipulated by the Royal Pharmaceutical Society (RPS) competency framework for all prescribers (Royal Pharmaceutical Society, 2021). This achievement enables them to engage in safe and effective prescribing practices. The learning outcomes of our programme have been carefully aligned with this framework, ensuring that learners are equipped with the necessary skills and knowledge to excel in their field.

The UEA IP programme operates on a continuous cycle, with three intake periods per year, spanning 26 weeks. In contrast, Institute B currently offers one intake per year that aligns with UEA's Term 2. Our programme is meticulously designed to cultivate a supportive learning culture and incorporates a blend of synchronous and asynchronous sessions. These sessions are thoughtfully crafted to provide a solid foundation of knowledge and understanding. Additionally, a diverse range of learning and assessment methods are incorporated to cater to the varied needs of our learners and promote lifelong learning. Irrespective of the institute, learners are expected to exhibit a thorough comprehension of the consultation process, pharmacology, and governance necessary for safe and effective prescribing decisions to successfully complete the program. The validation of our programme is dependent on both Higher Education Institutions (HEIs) ensuring an equitable learning experience for all learners.

The program is delivered online through the designated virtual learning environments (VLE) of the respective institutes, namely Blackboard and Moodle. As the course director, it is imperative for me to ensure that all learners have an equitable learning experience, regardless of the HEI they are affiliated with. This entails leading and coordinating the teams at both institutes to deliver the program with consistency and parity.

The Problem

The co-teaching structure of our programme, spanning two HEIs with differing VLEs, presents certain challenges. Each time the programme runs, the content must be transferred and synchronised across these two distinct VLEs. This duplication process involves creating materials in one VLE and then replicating them in the other. Consequently, there exists a logistical inefficiency in terms of administrative burden for content maintenance, ensuring parity when updates are made, and consistency in the learning experience.

An ideal solution would be to have a unified learning technology platform that serves as a single content repository accessible to both institutes. This would alleviate the logistical inefficiencies associated with transferring and maintaining content across two different VLEs. By having a central platform, administrative burden and content maintenance tasks would be streamlined, ensuring parity and consistency in the programme delivery.

This case study outlines our experience of identifying and implementing PebblePad as a digital technology solution to facilitate a collaborative and coherent approach to co-teaching across two HEIs. By leveraging PebblePad, we were able to create an equitable and user-friendly teaching resource that benefited both learners and instructors.

The Approach

Technology plays a crucial role in shaping our learning environments (Jones and Shao, 2011). In a Higher Education context, we have a wide range of digital technology tools at our disposal to support learners and enrich their educational journey. Virtual learning environments (VLEs) are adept at delivering teaching materials, resources, facilitating discussion forums, and managing assignments and grades. However, traditional VLEs have certain limitations when it comes to collaborative working and shared spaces between different institutes. In such scenarios, VLEs may not provide the necessary functionality to promote seamless collaboration and shared resources between institutes.

In 2021, we implemented the PebblePad platform as a solution for our learners to create electronic portfolios (eportfolios), thereby transitioning away from traditional paper-based practice assessment documents (PADs). PebblePad offers both the ability for educators to build and distribute resources that scaffold student activity, and a space for learners to collect evidence and reflect on their learning experiences over time (PebblePad, 2023A). One of the key factors that influenced our decision was the fact that both institutes had access to PebblePad. My experience of using PebblePad as an eportfolio tool led me to explore its potential in addressing the co-teaching challenges we were facing.

Consideration of Learning Experience Design (LXD) (Clark, 2021, Earnshaw et al., 2021, Floor, 2023, Jahnke, 2023) was a crucial aspect in the design of our content repository. LXD aims to empower learners in achieving their desired learning outcomes and, considering their unique preferences and abilities, to create a meaningful and effective learning journey

(Floor, 2023). In essence, LXD seeks to personalise the learning experience, ensuring that it is engaging, relevant, and impactful for each individual learner. Essentially, we want our learners to enjoy their experience of using the digital technologies we propose. The Venn diagram in Figure 1, taken from Earnshaw et. al. (2021), illustrates LXD as the intersection of the pedagogy and the technology with the social-cultural aspect. Our learners engage with multiple digital platforms throughout their learning journey. As they navigate through this journey, it is important for us to minimise the potential for cognitive overload.

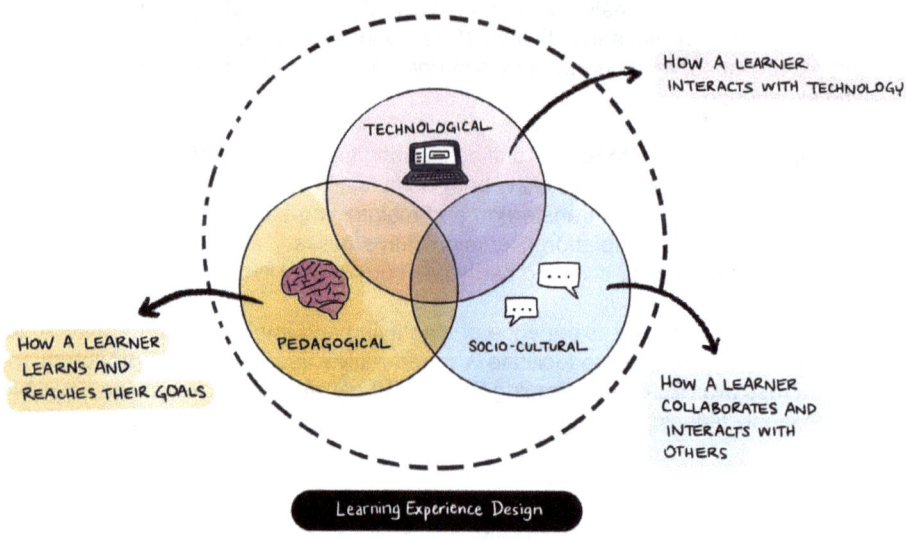

Figure 1: Three dimensions of LXD (Earnshaw et al., 2021)

By utilising PebblePad as a digital platform for both our teaching content and eportfolio, we can provide an integrated experience for our learners. This approach allows us to avoid adding to the cognitive burden for both our learners and staff, as they do not have to adapt to a new technology. It serves as an ideal solution in terms of streamlining the learning experience, ensuring parity and consistency in the programme delivery.

As a user interface, PebblePad is designed to be intuitive and easy to use, requiring only a minimum level of competency to get started. Its simple drag-and-drop functionality allows users to easily build content that can be linked to a workspace in ATLAS. Moreover, PebblePad provides scaffolding tools such as templates, interactive Workbooks, built-in frameworks, and activity logs that can assist learners in engaging in reflective practice (PebblePad, 2023B). As a team, we found it straightforward to tailor and adapt the portfolio features within PebblePad to create a teaching content workbook that effectively supports our learners. The flexibility of the platform allowed us to customise and align the features according to our specific teaching needs. This adaptability has proven beneficial in providing a tailored and effective learning experience for our learners.

The teaching content repository was meticulously prepared by creating a dedicated ATLAS Workspace consisting of a series of Workbooks corresponding to each week of teaching. To ensure a structured and paced delivery of content, these Workbooks were pre-set to be systematically released on specific dates. Within each Workbook, pages were added to represent the weekly content. Each week was thoughtfully structured in a consistent format, starting with an introduction page that provided an overview, learning objectives, and a list of activities to be completed during that week. To enhance the visual appeal of the Workbooks, PebblePad's extensive library of images was utilised to create eye-catching banners and images. Populating the content pages within the Workbooks with text, images, videos, and links was a straightforward process thanks to the user-friendly interface of PebblePad. This allowed for seamless integration of multimedia elements to enhance the learning experience.

Content was organised into distinct sections utilising various headings and subheadings within PebblePad. The platform offered a range of preset formatting options, empowering us to enhance the readability and structure of the content. This allowed learners to easily navigate through the material and locate specific information, fostering a uniformed and efficient learning experience.

The Results

We achieved the successful establishment of a comprehensive teaching content repository in PebblePad and piloted it in January 2023, with parallel intakes in both institutes. This repository was purposefully developed to enable both institutes to seamlessly access and update content, irrespective of their affiliated VLEs. PebblePad proved to be a viable solution to address this issue, after careful analysis of relevant research and personal reflection. With the successful completion of this project, we have achieved our goal of establishing a single digital platform for teaching content. This platform allows for easy accessibility and updating, ensuring that all institutes involved can benefit from the repository without any limitations imposed by their specific VLE. We are currently implementing our second instance of co-teaching for the parallel intake in 2024, and we are also utilising this teaching approach for all UEA intakes independent of co-teaching.

The academic standpoint of this accomplishment is significant, as it allows for the sharing and collaboration of teaching materials amongst multiple institutions. By breaking free from the constraints of individual VLEs, we have fostered a more inclusive and efficient approach to teaching content management.

One of the major advantages of using PebblePad is its visually appealing interface and user-friendly navigation. The platform's aesthetic appeal makes it visually pleasing, while its intuitive design enables easy and seamless navigation for users. By incorporating PebblePad in our teaching approach, we have succeeded in facilitating a high-quality learning experience for our learners. We have focused on understanding how our learners interact with technology and have effectively applied this knowledge to enhance their learning journey.

Overall, the implementation of PebblePad as a solution in building this teaching content repository has proven to be a success, and we look forward to the continued growth and improvement of this platform as we further enhance our academic endeavours.

> "So, using PebblePad, here's a much more level platform for their teaching content because it just means that any enhancements to the teaching content can be used by students at both sites. And so, there's much better equity in the student experience."
>
> Colleague Feedback

> "Each week we know what needs doing, great structure and well organised content."
>
> Learner Feedback

In the field of health sciences, the concept of 'person-centred care' holds significant importance. This term refers to the provision of support and assistance to individuals who utilize health and care services, enabling them to acquire the necessary knowledge, skills, and self-assurance to make well-informed decisions and actively participate in their own healthcare (Department of Health, 2013). Interestingly, we can establish a similar correlation between health professionals and those in academia with the concept of "student-centred learning".

Lessons Learnt

Initially, we looked to PebblePad as a pure content repository. We transferred existing content from the host VLE into a PebblePad Workspace. However, we soon discovered PebblePad offered further opportunities to enhance our learners' experience than we had initially realised. We found that by creating a virtual "Workbook" within PebblePad, we could not only refine existing material but also include new activities, adding spaces for reflection and note-taking. This greatly enhanced the design of the learning experience and benefited our learners.

During the process of building the course in PebblePad, we faced challenges with embedding specific interactive platforms. However, the responsive PebblePad support team quickly added the required platforms to their approved list, enabling us to incorporate interactive elements like quizzes into the Workbook. This helped to engage our learners and promote active learning.

PebblePad is not primarily designed as a communication tool for interaction between learners. Building in the social-cultural aspect of learner experience design required some creativity. To address this, we embedded Padlets, an online bulletin board, within PebblePad. Padlet provided a platform for learners to introduce themselves, share feedback, and partake in peer review activities throughout the program.

An additional feature that we did not originally consider was that PebblePad offers the opportunity to create legacy accounts for learners, allowing them to continue their professional learning after completing the program. This feature is highly beneficial.

As with any design process they are not static. Designs are always evolving. Improvements always sought and opportunities investigated to improve best practice based on evidence. Since the original build we have integrated PebblePad access within our host VLE, making it easily accessible for learners with just one click, no logins required.

The only barrier we were unable to overcome was the ability to teach synchronously through PebblePad. For this we are still reliant on our host VLE. However, despite this limitation PebblePad functions impressively as an asynchronous teaching platform.

In Brief

- Institutional defined VLEs restrict collaborative teaching opportunities across HEIs.
- Embrace creativity with digital technologies and leverage their unique strengths, even if it entails unconventional approaches.
- Place the learners' experience at the core of content creation and technology interaction to provide meaningful and interactive experiences to promote effective learning through technology.
- PebblePad can be utilised as a single point of truth to house communal teaching content alongside the institutional VLE platforms to facilitate co-teaching.

References

Clark, D. (2021). *[electronic resource] : Learning experience design how to create effective learning that works. Clark, Donald*, Kogan Page, Limited.

Department of Health (2005). *Nurse and pharmacist prescribing powers extended.*

Earnshaw, Y., Jahnke, I., Schmidt, M. & Tawfik, A. (2021). *Understanding the complexity of learning experience design* [Online]. Available: https://medium.com/ux-of-edtech/understanding-the-complexity-of-learning-experience-design-a5010086c6ee (Accessed: 9th August 2023).

Floor, N. (2023). *This is learning experience design: What it is, how it works, and why it matters*, New Riders.

General Pharmaceutical Council. (2022). *Standards for the education and training of pharmacist independent prescribers* [Online]. (Accessed: 10th July 2023).

Health and Care Professions Council. (2019). *Standards of proficiency* [Online]. Available: https://www.hcpc-uk.org/standards/standards-of-proficiency/ (Accessed: 4th July 2023).

Jahnke, I. (2023). *Quality of digital learning experiences – effective, efficient, and appealing designs?* The International Journal of Information and Learning Technology, 40, 17-30.

Jones, C. & Shao, B. (2011). *The net generation and digital natives: : Implications for higher education*, AdvanceHE.

Nursing and Midwifery Council. (2018). *The code* [Online]. Available: https://www.nmc.org.uk/globalassets/sitedocuments/nmc-publications/nmc-code.pdf (Accessed: 15th March 2023).

PebblePad (2023A). *PebblePad - the learning journey platform* [Online]. Available: https://www.pebblepad.co.uk/ (Accessed: 5th July 2023).

PebblePad (2023B). *PebblePad features* [Online]. Available: https://www.pebblepad.co.uk/features.aspx (Accessed: 11th July 2023).

8

Windows and Mirrors: a view into practice, the evolving professional capability of students and an invitation to examine our own reflection

Dr Linda Jaffray[1], John Cooper[1], Leigh Harkness[1], Kathryn Terry[1], Dr Yang Yang[2], Bob Wylie[2]

[1]School of Nursing, College of Health and Medicine, University of Tasmania, AU
[2]Digital Futures, College of Health and Medicine, University of Tasmania, AU

The Context

The Bachelor of Nursing (BN) Program offered by The University of Tasmania's School of Nursing aims to educate a new generation of nurses with capability in leadership and future-focused health care. Utilising a blend of digital and face-to-face learning and teaching, the program is delivered across four campuses. Three campuses are situated within the small Island state of Tasmania which comprises a population of 572,660, and one campus in a large metropolitan area of Sydney, New South Wales (NSW) with a population of approximately 5,297,089 (Australian Bureau of Statistics, 2023).

Professional Experience Placement (PEP), also known as clinical placements or work-based learning, is a core requirement of the BN Program. Placements enable students to put theory into practice, experience immersion and socialisation in real-world healthcare environments, and foster the development of an emerging professional identity (Berndtsson, et al., 2020; Houghton, 2014). Students are required to undertake a minimum of 800 placement hours throughout their degree to be eligible for registration with the Australian Health Practitioner Regulation Agency (AHPRA). Students complete five placements of between 2- and 7-weeks duration across varied healthcare settings and are supervised and assessed for competency by an experienced Registered Nurse (RN) in practice. Nurses in practice-based education roles are often referred to as Clinical Facilitators or Preceptors and are critical partners in educating the future nursing workforce.

The Problem

Historically, documenting placement-based learning and assessment had been paper-based. A document was printed, exchanged between students and their clinical facilitators, then scanned, and uploaded, post placement, into the Student Learning Management System for final review by Unit Coordinators. This paper-based approach to work-integrated learning and assessment was fraught with challenges, including lost or incomplete documentation, inefficient access to and exchange of assessment documentation, inability to monitor and respond to issues of student progression in a timely way, along with difficulty verifying assessor legitimacy. Additionally, paper-based processes do not afford efficient means by which to analyse student performance at scale.

Contemporary, digital solutions to assessing student learning in practice are increasingly advocated (Gray, Downer & Capper, 2019; National Health Service, 2018; Smith & Cambers, 2017). COVID-19 disruptions to both healthcare provision and higher education have accelerated the use of technology and created an impetus for cultivating a digitally capable health workforce (Dykes & Chu, 2020; Royal College of Nursing, 2018; Schwartz, 2019).

In 2021, recognising the need for a more contemporary, digital approach to placement assessment and the rapid uptake of technology in education and health landscapes, we undertook a digital transformation project. The project's aim was to redesign and transition work-integrated learning and assessment resources in the Bachelor of Nursing (BN) program from a static paper-based format to the contemporary, digital platform of PebblePad. Intended outcomes were to remedy the limitations of the previous paper-based approach, to leverage data functionality of digital assessment to generate timely and actionable insights to inform curriculum and quality improvement, and to respond to the increased needs of industry to prepare an adaptive, digitally capable, health workforce.

The Approach

Senior leadership in the School of Nursing and Digital Futures Team approved the employment of a 6-month, full-time Project Manager position, which was subsequently extended to 9 months to facilitate project completion. A cross-disciplinary project team was established. PebblePad was chosen as the contemporary learning platform in which to build and provide digital placement Workbooks for all undergraduate nursing students. A collaborative, staged approach was used to design and support the program-wide adoption of the new digital assessment process. Built within each stage were iterative feedback cycles that informed subsequent developments of the digital tools, associated resources, and process.

Stage 1: Early and Ongoing Stakeholder Collaboration

Early and ongoing stakeholder engagement was a primary consideration. Informed by the values of collaboration, respect, reciprocity and receptivity to feedback, the project worked in partnership with undergraduate nursing students, academic and professional staff, educational technologists, and practice partners, across two Australian states: Tasmania and New South Wales. A collective effort was required to develop and refine PebblePad Workbooks as comprehensive, structured feedback resources to cultivate and evidence students developing practice.

Stage 2: Two-phase Pilot and Preliminary Evaluation

Following the development and testing of the PebblePad Workbooks, a small-scale pilot occurred with a subset of students and their nursing facilitators (N=23) undertaking a three-week placement rotation. In phase two participant numbers increased to N=87 (n=67 students, n=20 nurse facilitators) from 35 different sites. PebblePad users were supported by a series of webinars and face-to-face trainings, along with purposefully designed PDF guides, screen recordings, and a dedicated email support account. Formal stakeholder feedback was sought through a 'Qualtrics' Online Evaluation Survey. Following a response rate of 50%, the digital placement Workbook and accompanying resources and processes were amended in line with feedback received.

Stage 3: Scaling-Up

The digital placement Workbooks in PebblePad were made available to the first 'full' unit cohort of 358 students undertaking a 6-week placement and their nursing facilitators (n=137). The 495 stakeholders were again supported by pre-placement webinars and a dedicated email support account.

Stage 4: Embedding and supporting adoption in the BN Program

PebblePad Placement Workbooks were embedded in all five placement units for use across the 14 placement rotations offered annually. In 2022 this amounted to supporting N= 3730 students, university staff and nurse facilitators in practice to engage with PebblePad Workbooks across the BN Program. Workflows were developed to support ongoing operational requirements for the set-up of digital Workspaces, the update and provision of PebblePad Workbooks, and the delivery of technical support and digital education.

The Results

Embedding PebblePad Workbooks as assessment resources for all placements in the undergraduate nursing degree has successfully achieved the projects intended outcomes of enabling timely and flexible access to placement assessment tools and resources by multiple users; real-time monitoring and response to issues of student progression; reduced inefficiency and mitigation of lost/missing Workbooks; and verification of assessor content and signature. PebblePad Workbooks have also been developed and implemented for pre-placement hurdle assessments, and pilots have just commenced in Postgraduate Nursing Courses which are characterised by a larger number of students who are more geographically dispersed throughout Australia.

Another important intervention outcome is the co-creation of new 'value-adding' PebblePad templates and resources with nurses in practice. For example, digital activities to cultivate skills in patient assessment, clinical reasoning, time management, shift-planning, patient documentation, interprofessional teamwork, and self-care have been developed due to the transformative partnerships cultivated throughout the project.

With the maturing of our PebblePad approach we now proactively use the data reporting functionality to generate timely and actionable insights into the student learning journey. This has provided the opportunity to not only gain a view into contemporary healthcare contexts and nursing expectations, but also to reflect on how we are preparing students for placement and practice. For example, based on data extracted from the Interim Review Assessment Activity in the PebblePad Workbook we identified the need to address student capability for receiving, and responding appropriately to, feedback. We were prompted to explore how students perceive and engage with feedback and, as a result, to design more explicit teaching about, and opportunities to practice, feedback skills. Additionally, these insights led to the creation of nursing narrative videos to model feedback literacy and skill. We have embraced the opportunity to reflect on our curriculum, it's areas of strength and opportunities for improvement, just as we ask of our students.

Lessons Learnt

This project has involved far more than the digitisation of placement assessment resources. It has necessitated consistent efforts to mobilise and sustain collaborative stakeholder engagement. Authentic attention to process, relationships and reciprocity continues to facilitate stakeholder collaboration to evolve placement-based learning and assessment design.

Transitioning to digital work-integrated learning assessment is not 'a set and forget' scenario, rather it's a dynamic, evolving space requiring sustained collaborative activity and forward thinking to anticipate and respond to changing requirements.

Project challenges have included bringing people together across traditionally siloed discipline, team, and organisational boundaries with diverse expertise and perspectives, navigating COVID disruptions, stakeholder stress and change fatigue, and varied levels of digital literacy. However, it has been a successful program of work due to several important factors. Enabling factors include senior leadership resourcing and support of a designated project lead, a cross disciplinary project team, early and continuing collaboration with key stakeholders as partners in health education, receptivity and responsiveness to feedback, and the willingness to reflect as a school on our strengths and areas for improvement.

In Brief

- Cultivating transformative partnerships within and across disciplines and organisational boundaries to reduce silos, develop trust, and harness diverse expertise is critical to digital transformation of placement-based assessment.
- Cross-disciplinary senior leadership support, and resourcing of a designated role to lead digital transformation projects, are key enablers of success.
- There is a need to build-in considerations for sustaining and evolving digital work-integrated learning resources and processes in response to rapidly changing education and healthcare requirements.
- Data analytics is a powerful functionality of PebblePad, providing a window into contemporary healthcare contexts and nursing expectations, the invitation to reflect on how we are preparing students for practice, and opportunities for these insights to inform curriculum development, quality improvement and innovation.

Feedback

Despite initial concerns of learning to navigate a digital system for student assessment in placement, feedback received from students, university staff and external healthcare partners have been over whelming positive. Early survey feedback attributed their positive experience of PebblePad placement Workbooks to the provision of targeted education, instructional guides, and in particular access to the prompt, empowering technical support and digital education.

More specifically, students have appreciated the creation of contemporary, comprehensive portfolios of evidence demonstrating their developing capabilities, with many now using this for the purpose of seeking employment upon graduation. Clinical Facilitators and Preceptors articulate a key benefit of digital placement Workbooks as supporting greater team-based facilitation and peer learning. From the perspective of university staff, the benefit of being able to view and respond to student issues in practice in a timely way is commonly cited:

> "…. to be able to jump in, in real time to see what is happening for students in practice and provide more timely support to them and their facilitating nurses has been a game changer."

References

Australian Bureau of Statistics. (2023, June). *National, State and Territory Population*. ABS. Retrieved from https://www.abs.gov.au/statistics/people/population/national-state-and-territory-population/latest-release.

Berndtsson, I., Dahlborg, E., & Pennbrant, S. (2020). Work-integrated learning as a pedagogical tool to integrate theory and practice in nursing education–An integrative literature review. *Nurse Education in Practice*, 42, 102685. https://doi.org/10.1016/j.nepr.2019.102685

Dykes, S., & Chu, C. H. (2020). Now more than ever, nurses need to be involved in technology design: Lessons from the COVID-19 pandemic. *Journal of Clinical Nursing*, 30(7–8), 25–28. https://doi.org/10.1111/jocn.15581

Gray, M., Downer, T., & Capper, T. (2019). Australian midwifery student's perceptions of the benefits and challenges associated with completing a portfolio of evidence for initial registration: Paper based and ePortfolios. *Nurse Education in Practice*, 39, 37-44. https://www.sciencedirect.com/science/article/pii/S1471595319301325?via%3Dihub

Houghton, C. E. (2014). 'Newcomer adaptation': a lens through which to understand how nursing students fit in with the real world of practice. *Journal of Clinical Nursing*, 23(15-16), 2367-2375. https://onlinelibrary.wiley.com/doi/full/10.1111/jocn.12451

National Health Service. (2018). A Health and Care Digital Capabilities Framework. NHS. Retrieved from https://www.rcn.org.uk/-/media/Royal-College-Of-Nursing/Documents/Clinical-Topics/A-Health-and-Care-Digital-Capabilities-Framework.pdf

Royal College of Nursing (2018) *Every Nurse an E-Nurse: Insights from a Consultation on the Digital Future of Nursing.* Retrieved from http://www.rcn.org.uk/professional-development/publications/pdf-007013

Schwartz, S. (2019). *Educating the nurse of the future—Report of the Independent Review into Nursing Education*. Retrieved from https://www.health.gov.au/resources/publications/educating-the-nurse-of-the-future

Smith, J., & Cambers, W. (2017). Using an electronic assessment system for nursing students on placements. *British Journal of Nursing*, 26(21), 1192-1196. https://doi.org/10.12968/bjon.2017.26.21.1192

9

From Literacy Skills to Skills Literacy: Supporting students' skills articulation through PebblePad as an eportfolio tool

Becky Lees, Barry Avery & Daniel Russell
Kingston Business School, Kingston University, UK

The Context

There is no doubt that modern university curricula have a greater focus on skills development now than in the past. At Kingston University we have developed the Future Skills programme recently discussed at the House of Commons; a combination of in-person workshops to help students understand the importance of personal development, along with the identification of nine graduate attributes, to be developed across the span of students' study programmes, building on experiences and skills at each level so they leave us as a professionally-skilled and in-demand graduate.

Within the Business School, we have taken this one step further by using PebblePad to capture students' skill and attribute development and as a platform where they can develop further skills of articulation and reflection. The end goal is for students to not only have the skills needed to do a job, but that they can also articulate them to future employers.

The Problem

Much of the literature around higher education skills development focuses on the importance of developing specific literacy skills such as information literacy, digital literacy, visual literacy etc. What is less covered, and what we are trying to address here, is students' "Skills Literacy", i.e.: their ability to articulate and think critically about their understanding of their own attributes and skillset and connect them to their own career plans, thus turning them into a resource for relevant graduate employability activity.

The literature is awash with all sorts of 'gaps' between higher education and the graduate market in the UK and internationally; digital skills gaps (eg: Taylor-Smith, et al., 2019), communication skills gaps in Australia (Moore & Morton, 2017), Canadian skills gaps (Brumwell, Deller & Hudak, 2019) to name a few. There is such a plethora of academic studies and stakeholder surveys, that the integration of skills in HE curricula is now a standard element of programmes of study. What is less explored is whether we are supporting students in learning how to articulate the development of these skills and attributes to the graduate market when they finish their studies.

Through our Future Skills approach, we believe we have a curriculum that integrates relevant skills for business and affords student opportunities to develop, test, and showcase these skills both inside the curriculum (e.g.: problem-solving to address client briefs in assessments, integrating professional certifications into programmes of study) and outside of the curriculum (Bright Ideas competitions to showcase creativity, internships and placements to acquire business experience). What we are now addressing is a possible 'skills articulation gap' (Watkins & McKeown, 2018; Kovalcik, 2019) whereby whilst students can complete activities to develop a skill or attribute, they are "lacking the tools to effectively communicate them to employers" (Watkins & McKeown, 2018, p.88).

The Approach

On our undergraduate business curriculum, students take between 12 and 14 academic modules, all of which integrate skills acquisition and opportunities for attribute development. As part of the assessment approach, students are also required to complete activities reflecting on their studies such as team logs for groupwork. However, we felt that our Learning Management System (LMS), with a focus on supporting learning and receiving assessment, didn't have the functionality we required to work as a large-scale single place where these reflections can be easily stored, organised and presented as a portfolio of skills.

To this end, we engaged PebblePad as a personal learning platform to act as students' personal space to collate and curate the evidence of their learning journey, as well as bring this all together to present a visual story of self. The benefit of PebblePad is that everything is in one place, and students can manage their assets, how and where they are used, and present themselves creatively to an external audience.

Guided by best practice principles regarding language, awareness, and contextualisation (Bowden, et al., 2000; Kovalcik, 2019), we developed a suite of structured online Workbooks to support students in first joining higher education, but also to help them navigate the longer-term collation of their experiences, artefacts and reflections that represent their learning journey. We decided to target our Workbooks at the holistic level, designed to support students in articulation rather than in demonstration of a skill acquired. In our initial pilot year, students therefore had three main Workbooks: KickStart 90+, Future Skills Workshops and Graduate Attributes.

KickStart 90+

This Workbook covered the induction period, including the first orientation week and the fortnightly personal tutor sessions in the first 90 days, focusing on developing institutional literacy through understanding the university discourse, processes, and assessment.

Future Skills – Workshops

This Workbook followed the activities students engaged in during their face-to-face personal development workshops integrated in each level of each programme. We started with the Navigate Workshops in the first year, and the Workbooks for the workshops in the second year (Explore) and final year (Apply) will be added at the start of the respective levels of study.

Future Skills – Graduate Attributes

This Workbook was designed to grow and provide a space for students to gather their evidence of developing the nine graduate attributes Kingston has identified as vital for graduate employment: Adaptability, Collaboration, Creative Problem Solving, Digital Competency, Empathy, Enterprising, Questioning Mindset, Resilience, and Self-Awareness. We included year one prompts (which will be repeated in years two and three) to get students to think about where they are acquiring skills through their first-year studies, links to extracurricular activities, and examples from sports and community activities. In this Workbook, we implemented the Collect-Reflect-Connect approach to support this development:

- **Collect**: students collect their evidence from activities they engage with in their studies, but also through work, volunteering, internships/placements, sports, home life or community engagement.
- **Reflect**: they then have space to reflect on what they learned, what worked or didn't work, and what they might do differently next time, using one of the structured reflective techniques (eg: STAR (Situation, Task, Action, Results), What? So What? Now What?) or their own reflective account.
- **Connect**: finally, they investigate why it's important for them to have this skill or attribute in the sector, role, or career path they wish to enter upon graduation, reflecting on industry requirements or desirable traits, and how they can showcase that they meet that need.

The Collect-Reflect-Connect activities are organised by level and include Skills Assessments so students can self-identify their strengths and areas for development amongst the nine graduate attributes. The aim here being to allow students to reflect on their growth in progressive years of their degree.

Previous studies recognise that reflection supports students' ability to link their experiences with identified skills (Tomasson Goodwin, et al., 2019; Maina, et al., 2022). By extending this process with the 'connect' step, the aim is to embed a regular process of linking back to abilities developed and articulating forward to how they will be used in industry, driving up awareness of what employers are looking for in different roles and sectors and thus reducing the skills articulation gap through a portfolio of increasing articulation and awareness.

The Results

We introduced the PebblePad platform across all first-year students on our business degree in a core class in the first year. To formally assess students' skill development, they have a Skills ePortfolio assessment in each year of their programme. As PebblePad was a new platform to most of our academic team and all of our first-year cohort, is was felt that using this for summative assessment during the introductory phase would be too challenging. However, we aligned the Future Skills – Workshops Workbook with the assessment and it became a formative space for students to try out their skills reflection before submitting for credit. We also get students to investigate job roles and career paths in the workshops so they can practice matching their skillset to what is needed in industry and begin developing the skill of articulation with the Connect activity in their attribute Workbook.

The academic tutors delivering the first-year modules identify activities in the curriculum where students can upload content or reflections to PebblePad to grow their evidence base for their attribute development, and as such student understanding of the platform and its objective is high given the direct link to their studies. We measured ongoing engagement statistics via the workspace to determine which in-class activities had the largest impact on the portfolio use and will be following up with module evaluation tools at the end of the year. Evidence to date shows students have engaged with the platform and have used it to structure assignment submissions related to employability skills in the curriculum.

We would argue that as students have engaged with PebblePad, they are more aware of the graduate attributes, their own skills, and the need for reflection than previously. The support from academic staff has been very positive and suggests that there will be further enhanced engagement in subsequent years.

Lessons Learnt

In hindsight it is easy to recognise the barriers we faced, and there are a number of lessons we learnt from our initial rollout. We underestimated the staff learning journey and the supportive role that a central team could provide. There was little resistance to the introduction of PebblePad given the central role the Future Skills project has at Kingston and the integration of the strategy across all strands of academic practice. Additionally, we thought there would be some issues with student onboarding, but they were very adaptable and with some personalised 'how to' guides and introductory videos, they have been active in using the platform.

Key to the success of launching the platform was identifying champions in key roles, and early adopters to facilitate. Bringing the course director and the module tutors together to discuss and identify ways in which we could integrate PebblePad into the course was crucial and resulted in course-level buy-in.

In Brief

As a pilot activity, our take-home messages are:

- Identify your allies – know who you need to get involved and onside to build the platform into the curriculum.
- Make it relevant and personalised – there is a balance to be had between commonality of Workbook content so you do not need to constantly update multiple versions when you want to make a change, and personalising the content to retain relevance to students so they can see why they should use it.
- Treat PebblePad like a social media platform in terms of regular classroom prompts, LMS signposts and emails reminding students of what content can be used in evidence for a skill or attribute development to keep students engaged.
- Always link to the discourse of the institution and industry – students need to make the link between what they can do and what employers want them to do, and it needs to start in year one and be explicit.

Feedback

Overall, the course team have been very positive about the introduction of an eportfolio tool to facilitate students' development of skills and attributes in a way which offers extended functionality over and above the traditional learning management system.

> *"The interactivity, personalisation and tangibility of the PebblePad platform offers us an opportunity to enhance the student experience around graduate employability."*
>
> Course director of Business undergraduate programmes

References

Bowden, J., Hart, G., King, B., Trigwell, K., & Watts, O. (2000). Generic capabilities of ATN university graduates. Canberra: Australian Government Department of Education, Training and Youth Affairs. Retrieved from: 04 May 2003 - Framework for Action - Trove, https://webarchive.nla.gov.au/awa/20030503164602/http://www.clt.uts.edu.au/Frameworkforaction.htm

Brumwell, S., Deller, F., & Hudak, L. (2018). The case for large-scale skills assessment. Driving Academic Quality: Lessons from Ontario's Skills Assessment Projects, *Higher Education Quality Council of Ontario*, Toronto, 53-64.

Kovalcik, B. C. (2019). Developing Employability Skill Articulation in College Students: A Framework and Practitioner Approaches for Co-Curricular Educators. *Journal of Campus Activities Practice and Scholarship, 1(2)*, 26-31.

Maina, M.F., Guàrdia Ortiz, L., Mancini, F. et al. A micro-credentialing methodology for improved recognition of HE employability skills. *International Journal of Educational Technology in Higher Education 19*, 10 (2022). https://doi.org/10.1186/s41239-021-00315-5

Moore, T. & Morton (2017) The myth of job readiness? Written communication, employability, and the 'skills gap' in higher education, *Studies in Higher Education*, 42:3, 591-609, DOI: 10.1080/03075079.2015.1067602

Taylor-Smith, E., Berg, T., Smith, S., Meharg, D., Fabian, K., & Varey, A. (2019). Bridging the Digital Skills Gap. In Proceedings of ITiCSE (Vol. 19, pp. 15-17).

Tomasson Goodwin, J., Goh, J., Verkoeyen, S., & Lithgow, K. (2019). Can students be taught to articulate employability skills?. *Education+ Training, 61(4)*, 445-460.

Watkins, E. K., & McKeown, J. (2018). The inside story on skills: The student perspective. *Driving academic quality: Lessons from Ontario's skills assessment projects*, 81-92.

10

Developing a multi-site, asynchronous assessment in a large, dispersed medicine course

Jennifer Lindley
School of Medicine, Monash University, AU

The Context

The medicine course at Monash University is a five-year program comprising two years of campus-based study and three years of hospital and community-based learning. The course is designed as an integrated curriculum structure comprising medical and behavioural sciences, sociology of health, clinical skills, ethics, and medical law.

The program is delivered across more than 20 locations in metropolitan Melbourne, regional Victoria and Malaysia, and includes clinical skills learning and assessment across all year levels. Student enrolments are approximately 500 students per year level with a total enrolment of around 2,500 students.

The assessment regime for the medicine course includes written and oral assignments, written examinations, and formal practical skills examinations, together with observation of patient encounters and completion of logbooks in the clinical workplace. PebblePad and PebblePocket are used for recording work-based tasks.

The Problem

At the end of the 2022 academic year the Faculty of Medicine, Nursing and Health Sciences at Monash University revised their approach to assessment to focus on authentic assessments together with improvements in feedback to students. As a result, the Monash School of Medicine held an Assessment Transformation workshop to review the program of assessment and guide decisions on the approach for assessment in 2023 and beyond.

A key element of the existing assessment for the course was the use of Observed Structured Clinical Examinations (OSCEs). These were formal end of year standardized, multi-station practical assessments with a scored performance. These examinations were high stakes and synchronised to be delivered simultaneously in centralised sites requiring dedicated space, sequestering of students, and many assessors. Criticisms of the OSCEs included significant implementation requirements, timed stations that encouraged poor clinical skill techniques, and delivery processes that created increased stress for students and assessors. Over the past few years, the approach for clinical skills assessment has been moving towards non-graded (pass grade only) competency ratings rather than scored results.

As a result of the new guidelines from the faculty and discussions at the workshops, the decision was made to remove the existing multi-station practical OSCE examinations and introduce new competency based clinical skills assessments for years 2-5 of the course. These assessments were to be introduced for the last campus-based year (Year 2) and all clinical year levels (Years 3-5).

The assessments were to be implemented as asynchronous, face-to-face, flexible competency-based assessments to be delivered to smaller groups of students. Campus based sites were to be used for second year and clinical sites for years 3-5. These sites are located across multiple metropolitan and regional sites in both Australia and Malaysia. Multiple attempts would be permitted for these assessments.

These changes were required to be completed within a tight timeline of just under 2 months in order to be ready before the start of the next clinical academic year.

The Approach

As PebblePad and PebblePocket had already been used for other work-based tasks, such as logbooks and patient encounters, students were already familiar with the platform and comfortable using their own devices. Using this platform, assessments could be undertaken anywhere at any time, which met the asynchronous, multi-site implementation requirements.

Our aim was to establish a set of cohesive, easily identified templates to record results of the required work-based assessments utilizing PebblePad and PebblePocket. The format of the templates was to be aligned across year levels with uniform layout, assessment domains and response options.

The key principles considered for this approach were based around the user experience and collection of assessment data. Essentially these principles were:

- User friendly format (least scrolling, least clicking).
- Standardised format for template file names.
- Standard wording for a competency-based rating of performance achievement across all year levels.
- Customized hints to inform performance requirements for each year level.

Students and staff were given guidance on how students could assist assessors to complete PebblePocket templates on the student's own device. On-line training was provided to assessors.

The Results

Using the PebblePad platform allowed the rapid implementation of the revised assessment approach across multiple locations. Standardised templates correlating to assessment rubrics provided a cohesive approach across year levels. Within the tight timeframe imposed, a system was implemented to deliver and record the new work-based assessment tasks across all sites.

Assessments were able to be undertaken asynchronously with each site taking responsibility for implementation for smaller groups of students in each session. The system allowed repeat attempts of assessments at a later date to reach the required standard. Reframing wording of response options to 'Nearly' or 'Not yet' for students who were not at standard addressed issues of 'failure to fail' where assessors were reluctant to return a 'Fail' result, which would result in a student failing to pass the entire academic year.

Instructions for the assessment process gave students responsibility for selecting the performance ratings and entering feedback in the template on behalf of assessors. Assessors were responsible for checking the entries then signing and locking the asset at the conclusion of the assessment activity. Feedback to students was provided during the assessment tasks and documented in templates, which allowed students to refer back and use this information for further learning.

The central assessment team for the medicine course were able to review ATLAS submissions to check on data from sites and provide monitoring and immediate support during assessment sessions. This ensured that forms were fully complete with results entered for each section of the template and that data was shared by students from PebblePocket to ATLAS. The real time monitoring of results and support to implementation staff facilitated immediate detection of missing data as well as rapid identification of those students who were not at standard and required additional learning support.

The inclusion in the templates of feedback fields to be completed during the assessment task increased access to documented feedback for students. In contrast to the formal OSCE assessments where students received a final overall result, they now have a record of their results and feedback for each assessment attempt in their PebblePad assets. This feedback can be used to guide additional learning for those students who did not achieve the required performance standard. Clinical academic staff have reported that they are able to quickly begin organising specific learning support for these students.

In 2023, more than 6000 assessments were recorded for almost 2,100 students across 15 assessment sites. Data for assessment outcomes was readily downloaded from ATLAS and formatted ready for inclusion in the university results management system. Analysis of assessment data will be used to inform quality improvement processes in design and implementation of this assessment approach.

While students did not receive feedback on performance in OSCEs, the preliminary data analysis for the new assessment process shows that quality of feedback to students needs improvement. Poor feedback included failure to provide or to record feedback, vague comments such as 'practice' or judgements such as 'good'. Constructive feedback included specific details on performance skills and recommended approaches to improve skills. This data will inform professional development for staff to build skills in providing specific and constructive feedback to students.

Lessons Learnt

The first implementation of this assessment approach revealed a number of barriers including:

- Academic stakeholders providing lengthy content for templates.
- Lack of clarity around template design requirements.
- Poor understanding of data handling.
- Continuous changes in staff using PebblePad.
- Student compliance with manual sharing from PebblePocket.

Key considerations for the next implementation are:

- Better communication with remote users.
- Improved training for new staff users.
- Improved template design to assist with data handling.

In Brief

- Establish a set of key principles for design.
- Engage with stakeholders for content and design.
- Consider naming conventions for templates.
- Real time monitoring provides key support for remote sites.

Feedback

A full evaluation has not yet been completed, however comments received indicate that the use of the PebblePad platform for high stakes assessment was generally well received.

Feedback comments from colleagues included:

> *"Definitely fit for purpose".*

> *"Provides good data management".*

> *"Real time monitoring and support was really valuable".*

> *"Easy to check on students at a particular site".*

> *"Able to quickly see which students needed further assessment attempts".*

Some areas of concern were noted:

> *"It feels awkward using a student's phone".*

> *"It's hard to type in feedback on a mobile".*

> *"A few students struggled with sharing assets (from PebblePocket to PebblePad)".*

11

Student organization event planning, review, and reflection: Workbook approvals, assessment data, and student leaders as Workspace Managers

Andrew Longhofer
School of Pharmacy, Pacific University, US

The Context

Doctor of Pharmacy students at Pacific University have formed ten different student organizations, with groups focused on specific practice specializations, professional development and advocacy, patient care and community service, social activities, and recognizing excellence in academic and leadership. A student governance group, PPSA, is composed of a generally elected Executive Committee (PPSA Exec), class officers for each cohort, and a representative from each student organization. PPSA is responsible for granting recognition and overseeing student organizations, allocating student fees to fund organizations and other activities that benefit the entire student body, and interfacing with the School's and the University's shared governance systems.

These organizations plan and hold a variety of events, ranging from simple get-togethers for their members, to large health fairs that provide members of the community with immunizations, blood glucose and blood pressure screenings, and education about medication safety, diabetes and cardiovascular disease management, and reproductive health.

The Office of Student Affairs (OSA) is responsible for setting and enforcing policies for student organizations, and for providing training, support, and mentorship to student leaders throughout their time leading these organizations.

Until 2023, Pacific University's PharmD program ran over three years: two didactic years with introductory clinical experiences between them, and then a year of six-week advanced clinical experiences. Students typically take leadership roles in their second didactic year. In 2023 we added the option of a five-year pathway, dividing the clinical years in half to provide flexibility for students to gain additional work experience or to accommodate family or community needs while working toward a professional degree.

The Problem

Student organization events represent a significant liability to the University and, when planned or executed carelessly, risk to the students involved. Pharmacy student organizations face particular legal and safety challenges due to the sensitivity of health information, the regulatory requirements for providing patient care, and the risk of harm to patients.

Historically, due to the rapid turnover of students in the three-year pathway, student organizations have struggled to maintain institutional knowledge from year to year. While student leaders are bright, ambitious, and highly engaged, many lack experience with event planning or risk management.

As we developed event planning and risk management procedures, we had several key priorities: providing scaffolding and support through the event planning process; facilitating officer transitions; ensuring thorough risk management practices and regulatory compliance; offering a space for reflection; and surfacing the learning and development that happens in the course of student leadership. Throughout, we sought to reinforce student governance autonomy within PPSA while still providing professional guidance from faculty and the OSA.

The Approach

PebblePad offered a single place to scaffold the event planning process, review and approve event proposals, capture the lessons learned, and create artifacts of students' achievements and the work that went into an event.

The Event Planning Workbook is structured to account for all the logistical considerations needed to plan an event. It begins with the basics (time, date, and location; who is responsible and who will serve as backup; the purpose and goals for the event) and proceeds through specific prompts related to budgets, patient care, transportation, contracts, food and beverage service, external guests to campus, and marketing and recruitment. A student who has never previously planned an event can open the Workbook, and by answering all of the questions in the Workbook, have made all the arrangements and have all of the information at hand in order to hold the event successfully.

After the event, the Workbook has a space for capturing the number of participants and community members served, any surprises (good or bad), suggestions for improving subsequent events, and feedback for the School on policies or resources that would have helped. At the end, there is space for reflection that can be marked as private.

Students submit the Workbook to an ATLAS workspace as soon as they begin planning so that the organization's advisor can monitor the planning process, offer comments or suggestions, and resolve any concerns or challenges that students encounter. Once event planning is complete, the advisor applies Approval Level One: red indicates that significant issues remain unaddressed; amber indicates that minor issues need work, but the event can proceed while those details are worked out; green indicates that the advisor is fully satisfied with the event.

The PPSA Exec then reviews the plan and applies Approval Level Two, with each color serving a similar function. PPSA Exec members are Managers of the Workspace - they navigate to ATLAS, apply approvals, and provide feedback themselves. While advisor approval primarily focuses on the event plans themselves, the PPSA Exec approval serves as a check that the advisor's concerns have been addressed and that the event does not conflict with other organizations interests. Both advisors and the PPSA Executive Committee have a feedback template available with a rubric to support their decision.

Finally, after the event, OSA reviews the event report page and applies Approval Level Three: red indicates that there was a significant safety or liability concern that must be investigated and resolved before the organization can hold another event; amber indicates that additional information is needed, but subsequent events can proceed; green indicates that the event report is satisfactory and represents a meaningful summation of the event and any lessons learned.

The ATLAS Workspace is set to allow all members to view all submissions in order to facilitate officer transitions and to serve as a repository of institutional knowledge to anyone planning an event later.

The Results

Through this process, every student organization event is held to the same standards of risk management and receives a consistent level of support. The feedback added by advisors and by PPSA Exec, when combined with the feedback student leaders capture on the Event Report page, has highlighted opportunities for OSA to provide better training and support to all student leaders. Disparities between advisor and PPSA Exec approvals have highlighted opportunities for further training and support for advisors.

Consistent review by PPSA Exec has also diminished schedule conflict between student organization events and increased their awareness and sophistication in peer enforcement of professional norms and standards. When advisors, PPSA Exec, or the OSA identify significant issues when applying approvals, or if an organization holds an event without approval, PPSA Exec is better able to exercise their oversight of student organization, and OSA can intervene when concerns about safety, legal liability, or individual students' conduct arise.

The ATLAS reporting suite has provided the School with the first meaningful usage and impact data on student organization events. While the number and variety of events is still recovering following the loss of momentum from COVID-19 restrictions, the data on events available through the ATLAS reporting suite has served to motivate student leaders to do more, more effective, and more engaging events than their predecessors. The School has begun to track this data to support our marketing initiatives and alumni relations, program assessment and accreditation, and fundraising efforts.

The Event Report has facilitated officer transitions by allowing students to pass down to their successors their ideas about improving annual event execution, and by making all submissions visible to all students, they can refer to them to work with contractors, caterers, community partners, and external guests that have been a part of previous events. The completed Workbook itself also becomes an asset that students can use as evidence as a part of our standardized competency assessment process for accreditation-required learning outcomes related to personal and professional development.

Perhaps the most important impact is that involving the Executive Committee as Managers of the Workspace has been the single most effective factor in creating buy-in for our PebblePad implementation.

Lessons Learnt

In order to avoid extraneous notifications, we used Sets and Manager permissions to limit notifications that advisors receive to only submissions from students in the organizations they advise. This works well; however, when a student in multiple organizations submits a Workbook, both organizations' advisors receive the notification. We have implemented a naming convention to help mitigate this limitation.

The first version of the Workbook used evidence blocks and linked templates for less common elements of the event planning process (a specific template for patient care events, for off-campus events, or for food and alcohol service). While this simplified the Workbook itself, it created issues for collaboration and for using the Workbooks in officer transitions when the individual templates were not shared. We reincorporated these templates as pages of the Workbook, and we introduced a checkbox list to direct completion and review instead.

Additionally, student leaders often struggled when their predecessors did not share their Event Planning Workbooks directly with them. We set up the Workspace through integration with a Moodle page that all students are enrolled in, so we were able to change the permissions to allow all Workspace Members to view all submissions; now, even if someone does not share a Workbook with their successor, the successor will still be able to consult it for future reference.

In the first few years, in order to report on participation and impact data, these were captured on the Event Report page using short text entry fields. Students would complete these in non-standard ways, requiring some manual data cleanup. With the introduction of reporting from tables, we were able to collect participation strictly as numbers, making this data much easier to report.

In Brief

- Using a Workbook to scaffold the event planning process can help student leaders plan events effectively regardless of their previous experience.
- Using feedback and approvals in ATLAS to review student organization event plans can improve consistency in risk management, oversight, and support.
- ATLAS can serve as an institutional repository for student organization event plans and reflections, facilitating officer transitions and serving as a resource for new student leaders.
- Giving student leaders Manager access to ATLAS enhances student autonomy and self-governance over student organizations, engages them fully as partners in institutional priorities, and builds buy-in for PebblePad implementation.

Feedback

Faculty advisors have appreciated the addition of rubrics to help guide their decisions in adding approvals. They also report that having all event details and conversations documented in one place, rather than spread across multiple documents and email threads, facilitates easier mentorship and support for students and a more comprehensive review when they are ready to approve the plans.

We have seen benefit from annual quality improvements on the Workbook and the workflow. However, some students have expressed frustration that, when there are major changes like going from evidence blocks for linked templates to incorporated template pages, they must start with a blank copy instead of making a copy of an event planning Workbook from last year and updating specific details.

Ultimately, engaging students as Workspace Managers has significantly de-mystified our intentions and rationale for adopting PebblePad, and by reviewing submissions and giving feedback in ATLAS, they have internalized the process for submitting assets for assessment and reviewing feedback in PebblePad. Upon the first meeting where event planning Workbooks were reviewed in ATLAS for approval, the student governance chair remarked: *"Now I understand why we are using this."*

12

Uptake and use of PebblePad Alumni Accounts by Australian graduates

Dr Jennifer Masters
PebblePad, AU

Themes

Employable and Future-ready, Professional Identity and Capability

Overview

As a teacher educator, I was passionate about evidencing learning through portfolios and the ongoing use of PebblePad. I actively encouraged my students to see learning as a journey that continued beyond graduation and throughout their career as a teacher. I loved that PebblePad provided Alumni accounts, and I ensured that students had every opportunity to set up their account for future use.

When I joined PebblePad as a Learning Support Specialist, I found myself on the other side of the process. My role in support means that I deal with the technical aspects of Alumni account creation. Creating an Alumni account is largely self-service, but we do get requests from students checking on the process and/or university IT support who are helping students to create accounts. We also get requests from graduates who didn't set up an Alumni account but then realise, occasionally years later, that their PebblePad work is important, and they want to access their content retrospectively.

This is an explorative research case study (Yin, 2017) of PebblePad Alumni account use in Australia over the last decade. It investigates the number of students setting up an Alumni account and explores the pattern of use after the account has been established. It also reports on the support tickets raised in association with Australian Alumni accounts and the outcomes of those requests. The findings from this study will help us to best support students in preserving evidence of their learning as they transition from university to the profession, and then their continued use of PebblePad to maintain a professional portfolio.

What is a PebblePad Alumni Account?

Anyone with a PebblePad institutional account can set up an Alumni account. This mechanism transfers ownership of assets from the institutional account to a PebblePad personal account. Usually, the option is suggested to students as they complete their studies and are ready to graduate. The student selects 'Free Alumni Accounts' from the Burger menu and then follows steps to create their personal account.

The advantage of the Alumni process is that the student will be able to continue to use PebblePad after they lose access to the University installation. Further, the university can delete the student's institutional account, freeing up their licence numbers, and the student's assets are safely stored in their personal account. The Alumni account is free to the student, and they will have unlimited use while their university has a PebblePad licence. If the licence is discontinued, they will have three additional years and then they can choose to take up a paid subscription for their personal account.

On paper, this option sounds like a great deal, and you might assume that most students would choose to hang on to their PebblePad account, even if they weren't sure if they would use it. This, however, doesn't seem to be the case.

What is the uptake of PebblePad Alumni accounts in Australia?

PebblePad has been in Australia for around 15 years and, while it was likely that Alumni accounts were available in some form in the early days, the earliest Alumni accounts on the current Pebble Personal AU installation were created in 2013. The average number of accounts added over the last 6 years has remained much the same, at around 1400 accounts per year. In total there are 12,240 Alumni accounts (at the end of November, 2023) (see Figure 1).

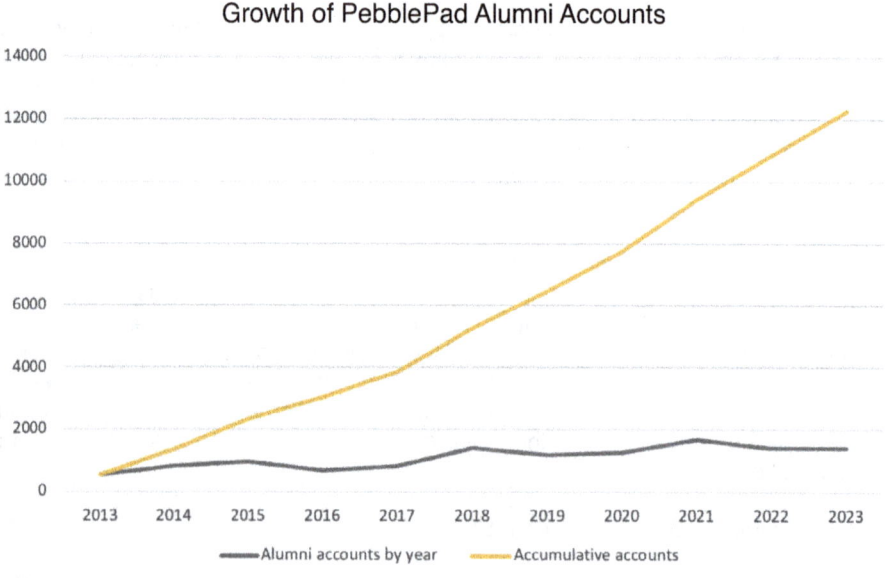

Figure 1: Alumni accounts in Australia

It would be difficult to ascertain the exact number of graduating students from our customer Universities in last ten years, but it is reasonable to guess that it would be significant. Many of our universities have enterprise licences with over 10,000 active users in a calendar year. Even if you allow for attrition, the lag of 3 or 4 years until graduation and the fact that universities have been progressively taking up PebblePad over the 10 years, you might recognise that the 12,240 students who have opted to create an Alumni account represent a small fraction of the students who have used PebblePad over the last ten years.

It seems that some universities are more proactive than others about encouraging students to take up Alumni accounts. PebblePad currently has 25 institutions as customers in Australia, and these range from large enterprise customers with over 20,000 active users in the last 12 months to small installations with less than 500 accounts. It doesn't appear that the Alumni accounts are distributed evenly according to the scale of PebblePad use, however. Figure 2 shows the distribution of Alumni accounts across the 25 institutions.

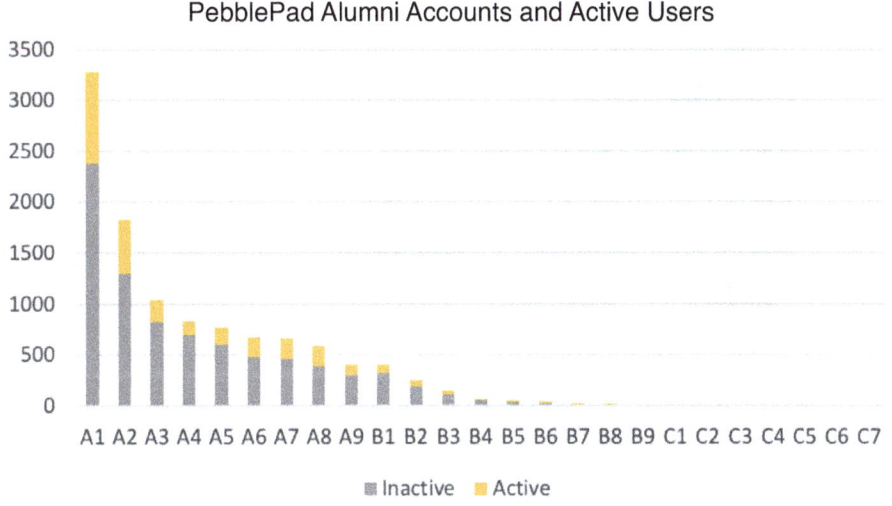

Figure 2: PebblePad Alumni accounts by institution, showing active and inactive users

Quite a few customers have only started using PebblePad in the last 3 years and so have few Alumni transitions as yet, however, it is evident that some universities with eligible graduates actively engage with the Alumni process, while others are less proactive. As an example, in Figure 2, the university coded A1 generates almost twice the number of Alumni accounts than any other university. They are an enterprise customer and have been using PebblePad for a large part of the 10 years, but then both A2 and A3 are similar in size and period of use, and they activate far fewer Alumni accounts.

The number of active Alumni Accounts from each institution is also shown in Figure 2. This study uses the definition of an 'active' user as having logged in more than 3 times. This does not indicate an extensive use of the Alumni account, but it does distinguish it from accounts that are created and then not used, or those that are only logged into once or twice. It was interesting to note that the ratio of active to inactive accounts was similar, regardless of the numbers from each institution.

Only 20-30% of students who create an Alumni account progress to active, with the average conversion of 25%. This means that 75% of Alumni accounts that are created are not really used.

So, do any graduates use their Alumni accounts for professional purposes? It appears that some do, although the percentage is quite small. Figure 3 shows the breakdown of use.

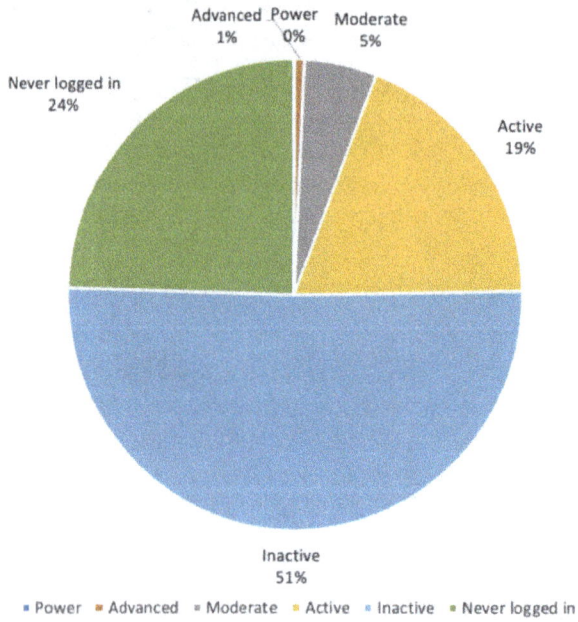

Figure 3: Use of Alumni accounts in Australia, based on the number of logins

Figure 3 confirms that 75% of Alumni accounts created are either not logged in to or only opened a few times. The active users have been segmented into active use (>3 logins), moderate use (>10 logins), advanced use (>40 logins) and then 'power' use (>200 logins). There were only 6 in the power use category, so not enough to register a percentage on this chart.

It is quite feasible that students in the moderate, advanced, and power use categories are using their accounts for professional purposes. As an example, once someone has created a professional portfolio, it might be that they only need to login a few times a year to refresh and keep it up to date. Accounts from these three categories represent 6% of all Alumni accounts.

What are the support issues for Alumni accounts?

When a student moves their content from their student account to an Alumni account, they transfer to the PebblePad personal installation and technically become a PebblePad customer, rather than a student of the university. There is, however, a transition period where the University may need to help the student transfer over. Consequently, tickets relating to Alumni issues may come directly from the user or from IT support at the corresponding university.

In a 12 months period (Nov, 2022 – Nov, 2023), the PebblePad support desk received 561 support tickets from Australian customers and 70 of these related to Alumni issues or queries (14%). A thematic analysis (Braun & Clarke, 2006) of these tickets produced 10 themes, as shown in Figure 4.

Australia Alumni Tcket Topics

Topic	Count
Successfully set up Alumni account, but can't see University content	11
Set up an Alumni too early	1
Link sent to students is damaged	7
Didn't set up an alumni account – uni activated retrospectively	8
Didn't set up an alumni account – uni account deleted	12
Customising the Alumni process	2
Confusion over login details or URL	14
Clarifying how an Alumni account works	3
Change of email or username	3
Alumni didn't create properly or is broken	8

Figure 4: Themes of Australian Alumni tickets over 12 months

Many of these tickets were not true technical issues, but rather they were seeking advice on how the Alumni account worked and where to find content. Importantly, a good proportion of the tickets (n=20, 28%) were queries about/from students who didn't set up an Alumni account when they left their university and were trying to recover their work retrospectively. Some of these students seemed to be aware of the Alumni process:

> "I used PebblePad at University over 2021-2022. I have since graduated and was informed that we would be invited to have access to our PebblePad as an Alumni but didn't receive this invitation."

Others, however, seemed to expect that they would just be able to continue to login via their university installation after graduation:

> "I am trying to access my PebblePad. I used it for Uni however it is saying it is now locked. I am wanting to access it, as it has lessons as a teacher that will be useful."

> "I haven't had access to PebblePad in a few years. Now I am trying to login again and it is showing me an error message."

This student had obviously heard about Alumni accounts but hadn't realised that there was a process for setting it up:

> "When at University I created a PebblePad which we were told we had lifetime access to. I am unable to log in to my account and was hoping you could help me."

While students are expected to create an Alumni account before they lose access to their university account, all might not be lost if they fail to do this. PebblePad provides a mechanism for the PebblePad administrators at the institution to initiate an Alumni account on behalf of the student. This only works, however, if the student's account is still exists in the university installation. If the account has been deleted by the university, then there is no content that can be moved across to an Alumni account – the student's work is lost.

It is very difficult to have to break this news to past students who come to realise too late that evidence of their learning is a valuable commodity. From the 20 tickets in this analysis where an Alumni account wasn't created, 8 were able to be set up retrospectively, while 12 were lost (see Figure 5).

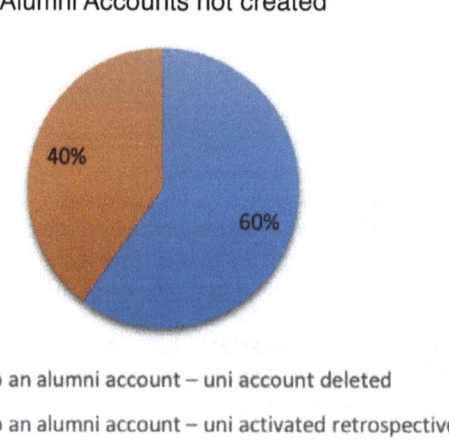

- Didn't set up an alumni account – uni account deleted
- Didn't set up an alumni account – uni activated retrospectively

Figure 5: Percentage of Alumni accounts that were retrieved retrospectively

Even though a student's PebblePad account is deleted, it is still possible to retrieve assets that have been submitted to a PebblePad workspace as pdf documents. This is a mechanism to preserve submissions for archiving and/or auditing purposes. When we ascertain that an account has been deleted and an Alumni account is longer an option, we suggest that the University can retrieve any assets submitted and then email the pdfs through. This is a poor consolation compared to a live and ongoing PebblePad account, but most graduates are grateful for at least some record of the evidence they produced as students.

Discussion

The advantages of students moving across to Alumni accounts at graduation are considerable. If a student has been using PebblePad consistently during their studies, they are likely to have accumulated a significant volume of evidence of learning, ranging from their very first attempts to capstone works, that represent the expanse of their professional knowledge at the cumulation of their study. Even if the student doesn't want to share their artefacts with others, they might use them to reflect on what they know and what they might want to share with others for professional purposes, for example for professional registration or a job interview.

A PebblePad Alumni account isn't just an archive of work. The graduate can continue to use the creative tools in PebblePad to build ongoing professional content. While there are a number of free online content builders, eg, Word Press, it is unlikely that these tools will provide the ad-free, secure context afforded by PebblePad. Further, PebblePad is very easy to use compared to other tools, which often require some html understanding. Bespoke PebblePad pages and portfolios can be created for any professional purpose, providing a sharable links that can showcase digital evidence, including images, video, presentations, embedded web apps and documents. These links are live, so the pages can be adjusted and updated after the link has been sent. It is also possible to restrict the time of the share, giving the developer control over who sees what and for how long.

Given that Alumni accounts are useful, free to students and require very little effort to set up, why is it that so many don't set up their account? This is a good question for further research - it would be fascinating to ask graduating students why they do or don't take this opportunity. It may just be that the timing is not ideal. As students reach the end of their degree, they are focused on completing all hurdles and assessment so they can finish with study. Their priority is on getting everything done, and they might feel that they never want to see a PebblePad asset ever again! It also could be that they are really busy, and that they either miss the instructions given to them to create an Alumni account or that they just don't get around to doing it.

As shown by the tickets we receive, some graduating students only realise how valuable their evidence is after they graduate. While some universities provide an extended period for student access to email, e.g. 6 months, many students lose their university access almost immediately, and this includes being able to login to PebblePad. It is likely that most students give up when they find that they can no longer access their account, but for those who persevere and manage to contact either their university or PebblePad support, not being able to login isn't such as huge issue, as the Alumni account can be created retrospectively as long as the account hasn't been deleted. Unfortunately, an institution will eventually need to remove historical accounts to free up accounts for new students and the longer a graduate delays creating an Alumni account, the more chance there is that their work has been purged.

Transitioning students to Alumni accounts is a partnership between the University and PebblePad, and it is likely that changes can be made from both perspectives to improve the uptake. As a starting point, it would be interesting talk to customers to find out what they are doing to promote Alumni accounts. For example, we might ask the PebblePad management team at university A1 how they encourage students on this pathway. It is obvious that they do have a strategy, as their numbers are significantly more than the other Australian universities. It would be beneficial to share strategies between universities. Simply highlighting the advantages of an Alumni account to both students and staff and suggesting some ways to facilitate the process may make a difference to universities who currently don't actively encourage students to take up this offer.

It is possible that PebblePad can do more to make Alumni conversion easier and more streamlined for students. The process is self-serve and is activated via the Burger Menu, but there are quite a few steps with written instructions that may discourage students to commence or complete the process. Students also need to begin the process in PebblePad but then follow instructions emailed to them. Any delay or distraction in the sequence may lead to the process being put off for another day or abandoned completely. While there are good reasons for not making the Alumni conversion process automatic, a review of the process and the support materials may make a huge difference to the uptake that we see across institutions.

Summary

It makes good sense for a graduating student to take up the offer of a free PebblePad Alumni account, but we know that only a small minority of graduating students in Australia convert their student account to an Alumni account. Further, even though the number of PebblePad users has increased dramatically over the last 10 years, the numbers of graduates creating Alumni accounts hasn't increased, with the number of new accounts flatlining over the last 6 years.

It may be that an overhaul of the Alumni system in PebblePad, along with better promotion and communication would make a huge difference to how many students choose to take up this option. This initiative is likely to lead to improved outcomes for graduates, helping them to retain evidence of their learning and continue to use PebblePad for professional purposes.

References

Yin, R. (2017). *Case Study Research and Applications: Design and Methods* (6th Edition). London: Sage.

Braun, V. & Clarke, V. (2017). Thematic Analysis. *The Journal of Positive Psychology Vol. 12 Issue 3*, pp. 297–298.

13

Student-Led, Individually-Created Courses (SLICCs): A reflection-based experiential learning and assessment framework using an eportfolio, scalable to support institutional Curriculum Transformation

Dr Gavin McCabe[1] & Professor Simon C Riley[2]
[1]Careers Service, The University of Edinburgh, UK
[2]Edinburgh Medical School, The University of Edinburgh, UK

The Context

The SLICCs initiative has emerged from a number of drivers, with the consistent aim of delivering student-led and credit-bearing experiential learning at scale.

At the outset: There was a strong interest from a range of staff across the institution, in different schools and disciplines, to find ways to support students in taking ownership of their own learning, and to support staff in providing effective reflective experiential learning and assessment, and in harnessing portfolios. Although there were already examples of such activity being very successfully implemented in individual courses, or with a specific disciplinary or vocational approach, these were typically not readily adaptable or scalable. While well established, characterised, and validated within their discipline, the discipline-specific nature of these approaches often made it a challenge to embed them in other fields without that established validity and the accompanying confidence to implement.

Subsequently: A large-scale, institution-wide Curriculum Transformation Programme emerged after the initial SLICCs work. This programme gives focus to the importance of continuing to evolve learning and teaching and maintaining the relevance of higher education. It aims to enable our students to develop self-regulated learning skills (Russell et al., 2022), to have confidence within an increasingly complex and uncertain world, full of difficult 'wicked' problems to address, that involve cross-disciplinarity, a divergency in values across different stakeholders, and no 'correct' answer due to their complexity and uncertainty (Head, 2009; McCune, et al., 2021). The Curriculum Transformation Programme is ongoing, gaining substantial momentum, and is now beginning to enter phased implementation.

The Problem

In response to these drivers, from the outset the SLICCs initiative identified key principles and approaches to consider, including:

- Enabling student agency.
- Shifting the focus beyond accrual of knowledge to delivering, supporting, and assessing a wider array of graduate attributes.
- Incorporating portfolio learning.
- Supporting students to undertake interdisciplinary work and to be able to work successfully in diverse teams.
- Increasing co-creation of learning.
- Providing safety for experimentation and learning from experiences that may be perceived as mistakes.

The core challenge was how to enable such student-led and experiential learning at scale, using limited resource, yet creating a meaningful experience for both students and staff?

The Approach

The overall approach

From the outset, we aimed to create a generic, flexible, and scalable reflective experiential learning and assessment framework, incorporating an eportfolio and usable by staff across the University. By centralising our initial development and ongoing maintenance and enhancement of the framework and supporting resources, we aim to enable staff to focus on delivering meaningful and engaging learning experiences and avoid having to develop learning resources, etc., and to enable students to have a high-impact experience that supports multiple student experience priorities.

The details

In some ways the SLICCs framework can be considered as an empty course, filled with activity and experience and structured by reflection. In it, we define the process to receive academic credit, the learning outcomes, and the assessment criteria. There is then a great deal of flexibility for the student, or a staff member as a course organiser, to define the activity on which the SLICC and the reflective journey will be based. The students themselves then take ownership of their learning journey through this defined activity and what they want to gain from it. Students contextualise the generic SLICC learning outcomes to their planned activity and specify how they will demonstrate completion of these by collecting and curating a range of reflective evidence in a structured workbook.

Students are supported by a comprehensive set of online resources, and by a tutor who offers structured formative feedback at the initial Proposal phase when students are taking ownership of their learning outcomes and learning journey, and then again at an Interim Reflective Report. The Interim Reflective Report is a draft of the Final Reflective

Report that is summatively assessed by the tutor and self-assessed by the student using the same assessment rubric as the tutor.

The generic learning outcomes have emerged as a key element to the success of SLICCs. We have created a framework of these learning outcomes to support different stages and levels of study, across the undergraduate levels from foundation and pre-honours to honours, and across postgraduate levels from masters to professional doctorates. The learning outcomes retain a core structure but are stratified with relatively minor changes in the wording incorporating complexity, uncertainty, criticality, and autonomy. There are five learning outcomes that at each level of study focus on:

1. Analysis of a main topic and its critical understanding developed through the student's activity.
2. Application of a broad range of academic, professional, and personal skills required to successfully engage in the activity and SLICC.
3. A Specific skill actively recognised and developed throughout the student's activity.
4. A Specific mindset actively recognised and developed throughout the student's activity.
5. Evaluation by the student of their overall approach, learning, and development throughout their SLICC, and implications for their future.

The specific skill and mindset are linked directly to the University's Graduate Attributes.

We started small and piloted on a quite limited scale in pre-honours although importantly these pilots were cross-disciplinary from the start. The initiative grew from there, continuing to develop and improve the support for students and staff, while continuing to retain the scalability and flexibility. During these pilot stages we established oversight by the Senate Sub-Committee supporting academic regulatory and governance requirements, so these were all fully and robustly addressed from the inception. We initially worked with staff who already had some level of confidence in experiential and reflective learning to establish trust and confidence in the approach. We then recruited the early adopters, who were interested in the approach and considered it to be a way to address a course design need of their own. What has become increasingly apparent is that on setting out to develop a flexible framework for reflective experiential learning, it has proved to be valuable in more flexible and creative ways than we could have ever envisaged. We are continuing to actively develop a community of practice where staff can support each other, including in partner institutions interested in implementing SLICCs themselves.

We have housed the whole process in PebblePad and ATLAS and have created all the support documents in PebblePad to maintain a consistent platform and format for both students and staff.

The Results

Student impact

From initial piloting and throughout rollout we have seen consistent gains for students in: enhanced skills; increased reflective ability and self-awareness; opportunity to connect past and present learning experiences; developing their mindset towards learning; increasing their assessment literacy; achieving deeper and more diverse learning from their activity; valuing the opportunity to safely experiment and learn from mistakes without academic detriment; and their autonomy and agency, including to be able to develop the capabilities and skills they deem to be valuable (Murray, 2023).

Staff impact

In addition to staff valuing the student gains seen, staff have particularly appreciated: the opportunity for meaningful and personal engagement with students' experiential learning; the academic rigour of the approach; and the freedom to focus on establishing rich and meaningful student activities because the learning and assessment approach is fully supported by the SLICCs framework and accompanying resources.

Scalability and institutional impact

The SLICCs framework is now used by over 30 courses across all three of our Colleges and in multiple schools, covering every level of study. The flexibility and success of the framework, and the alignment with institutional priorities, means SLICCs are now firmly embedded in the range of approaches being harnessed by the institutional Curriculum Transformation Programme. Additionally, SLICCs have also significantly influenced some local initiatives that have adopted elements of the approach, opening up an understanding of effective reflective learning and its assessment.

In Brief: key challenges and success factors

Design: scalable but resource-light and positive impact for all involved

- Drawing on past experiences and expertise around resource-light but high-impact scalability, for example our Edinburgh Award (www.ed.ac.uk/edinburgh-award).
- Establishing a scalable model from the outset, and maintaining a focus on efficiency and impact as we continue to enhance and develop the offering.

Attitudes: overcoming uncertainty and the focus on assessing knowledge

- Phased piloting as staff and institutional confidence built in awarding credit for this type of learning.
- Recognising importance of knowledge, but maintaining a constant and deep focus on using reflection to assess attribute development, with extensive support for students and staff: Reflection Toolkit (www.ed.ac.uk/reflection).

Flexibility and agility: providing solutions to current and future challenges

- Focusing on the underlying learning process and investing to keep it fully generic.
- Establishing a tested and ready-to-go framework and supporting resources that solve local curriculum design challenges and a staff need.
- Highlighting alignment with the emergent institutional vision to support our future students' learning and preparedness to deal with significant challenges in our complex world.

Feedback

Feedback has been resoundingly positive from students. They say that it is an important motivator:

"I think it helped motivate me to take the initiative in following and researching my personal interests, and then expanding on that so I can produce something of my own."

And that it becomes transformative in the way they view their approaches to learning:

"The reflection really helped highlight the learning techniques that work best for me."

"I feel like my whole attitude to learning has changed because of the process."

Staff also report a rich series of positive elements including recognising how the approach develops students' ability in reflection and increased self-awareness, connecting past and present learning experiences, while developing a 'mindset for learning' and their assessment literacy. SLICCs enable deeper and more diverse learning from students' experiences and further enhance students' wider toolkit of skills. Staff also particularly see the benefit of an approach that allows students to make mistakes, but in learning from them students can still get a top grade.

References

Head, B. (2008). Wicked problems in public policy. *Public Policy, 3(2)*, 101–118.

McCune, V., Tauritz, R., Boyd, S., Cross, A., Higgins, P., & Scholes, J. (2021). Teaching wicked problems in higher education: Ways of thinking and practicing. *Teaching in Higher Education Critical Perspectives, 28(7)*, 1518-1533.

Murray, R. (2023). The capability approach, pedagogic rights and course design: Developing autonomy and reflection through student-led, individually created courses. *Journal of Human Development and Capabilities*. https://doi.org/10.1080/19452829.2023.2261856

Russell, J.M., Baik, C., Ryan A.T., & Molloy, E. (2022). Fostering self-regulated learning in higher education: Making self-regulation visible. *Active Learning in Higher Education, 23(2)*, 97-113.

14

Using PebblePad for authentic assessment in ways that might not have been envisaged

Paul McLaughlin
School of Biological Science, The University of Edinburgh, UK

The Context

Our use of PebblePad is for pre-Honours undergraduate student cohorts of 80-400 in a STEM discipline (Biology) in a large University. Like many others, our curriculum is placing increasing emphasis on experiential and reflective learning. The first and second years of our new curriculum have, and are being, implemented. These students will have higher expectations when they come to our largely still unmodified third year. Therefore, in the third-year course, we are very mindful of providing authentic learning opportunities and supplying feedback in a timely manner.

The Problem

Biology is becoming more of a "Big-Data" subject, evidenced by genome sequencing projects. As an example, to identify the micro-organisms in a pond, nowadays a biologist does not look down a microscope, with the "Observer Book of Pond Life" in the other hand. Rather they sequence the DNA present and use data science methods to find out which organism were there by matching to large databases holding previously annotated records.

In a wider sense, we wanted students to find out information for themselves, using publicly available web-servers that their teachers would use in their own research. To us it was more important that they learned from the process of finding out how to use unfamiliar software than that they learned to use any specific one. We also wanted the students to experience a narrative by looking at the same problem through a variety of lenses (web servers) that built an increasingly deep picture. As far as possible we wanted our narrative to follow that of the course so that what was being learned in lectures could be tried in practice. Finally, we wanted to ensure that the students got timely feedback within a week so that they could feed-forward to the next exercise.

The Approach

Each student was given their own complex containing two different proteins. In a PebblePad Workbook, they were given a task each week to find data on their unique complex using a different website, and looking at a different aspect each time (Figure1).

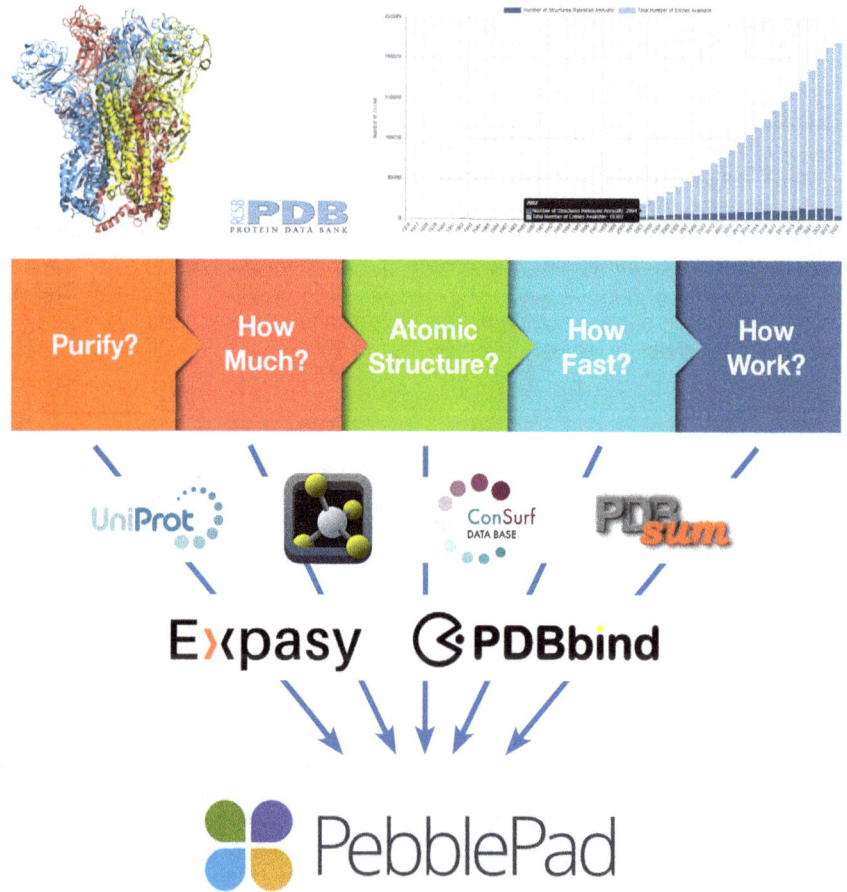

Figure 1: An example of a protein complex (Covid Spike Protein), one of many different complexes in a publicly available data bank. Students are given a different one each, answering increasingly sophisticated questions each week using the web servers illustrated, the results of which are aggregrated in PebblePad.

To ensure we gave rapid feedback, we downloaded the student responses into a csv file. This was read into an Excel file containing the answers, which in turn had been 'data scraped' using the APIs supplied by the websites. Rapid feedback could be constructed by using macros within Excel (Figure 2).

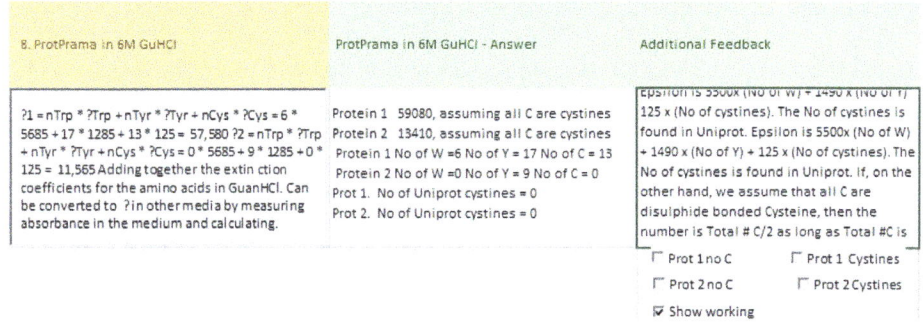

Figure 2: The student answer (left) is shown beside precalculated/ data scraped answers (Middle). Check boxes (right, lower) insert feedback right(upper). These are aggregated for each question and finally pasted into the feedback tab on PebblePad for the submitted asset.

A marker gets the student response and expected feedback side by side, next to pre-computed feedback that can be selected from checkboxes, which in turn apply the mark for each question. In this way the amount of reading by the marker is reduced since all the detail intended for the student is removed and only the essentials are shown. No calculation of mark totals is needed. Nonetheless, fields are made available for markers to type their own feedback for cases that pre-calculated feedback did not envisage, and markers have control to change marks if they wish. The main design principle was that markers should concentrate on the students' work with the minimum of distraction, yet still with flexibility to have agency.

Feedback was aggregated into a paragraph and then uploaded back to PebblePad, into the student's Feedback Tab. Originally the marker had to paste this for each student. But we subsequently worked out how to do this automatically "as a gang" (Selenium), which freed up a marker to go straight to assess the next student.

The ability in PebblePad to download all student work as a csv file was crucial to this work. We can also make direct links to student's submitted image file (downloaded from PebblePad). Not many assessment engines have these capabilities. Thereby agency is given to teachers to develop strategies that the developers may not have envisioned. A hope is that such "string and sealing wax" experimentation may be a proof of concept that the developers may incorporate into the platform.

Similarly, PebblePad's trust in academic users allowed us to provide rather sophisticated Peer Feedback. We managed to arrange that pairs of students anonymously gave feedback to another pair of students, and then the assessing students could check their own feedback against their partner's feedback. Judicious use of sets in PebblePad, and adaptive release of links in our VLE, were key. As a result, not only did students learn to gauge their own work against others, but they also learned to gauge the quality of their own feedback against another.

The Results

The exercise has run successfully for four years now. In the initial years, the Excel marking sheet went through a lot of development and bug-fixing. As a result, in the earlier years we did not always make our one-week target. But the development is now mature, and we do make that target. The exercise is appreciated by students because they get a feeling of "doing" their subject, rather than being told what to learn and what to believe. It is a constant that gives them a sense of progression. Some students mention that through doing the exercise they see how the course fits together, as more than the sum of its parts.

The peer feedback component has run successfully with large classes of 400+ students.

Lessons Learnt

In retrospect, developing the Excel spread sheet took too long. Nevertheless, the total saving in time is increased by every subsequent year it runs. The biggest barrier was bringing along academic colleagues who would do the marking. Extra marking during term time is never welcome, so they had to be convinced of its worth. The aim was that feedback for 80 students should take roughly 3 hours. In retrospect, more time was spent ensuring markers had a good experience, and so would continue supporting the exercise, than was expended on the student's experience. An unanticipated problem was that some macros, developed on Windows, did not work on Mac computers. Eventually we learned what would work on both. The process has been improved by feedback from the academic markers and best practice has been incorporated. Perhaps we are at a stage that soon teaching assistants could take over, but it would be a shame that those giving lectures would lose this opportunity for their own feedback on what students understood and could do.

A final reflection is that the sustainability of an innovation requires thought. Is there an exit strategy for the developer? The whole system needs to be documented and made usable by support staff, otherwise the developer's own workload remains high (and workload models do not compute these tasks). But if these problems were anticipated, there would never be any innovation.

In Brief

- Colleagues need to be taken along, so trust your instincts about what they will bear in giving feedback and try to make their experience as minimally frustrating as possible.
- PebblePad's open structure, together with careful implementation that does not limitpossibilities, allows for innovation.
- PebblePad can be thought of as an assessment engine in itself, not only as a platform for reflection.

Feedback

Extended Portfolio

"The portfolios are lovely"

"Portfolio is great! It is also informative"

"Portfolios 😊 😊 "

"With each portfolio looking at specific interaction characteristics, I was able appreciate the different types of analyses used to investigate these in more depth than I otherwise would have if I had done it all at once in a traditional course project."

"Having them all in the same workbook on PebblePad made it much easier to look back at previous work, other in-course assessments, and feedback on those to improve my subsequent submissions."

"I am able to look back at the instructions and background information used in the portfolios and apply these to other proteins I study in the future."

Peer Feedback

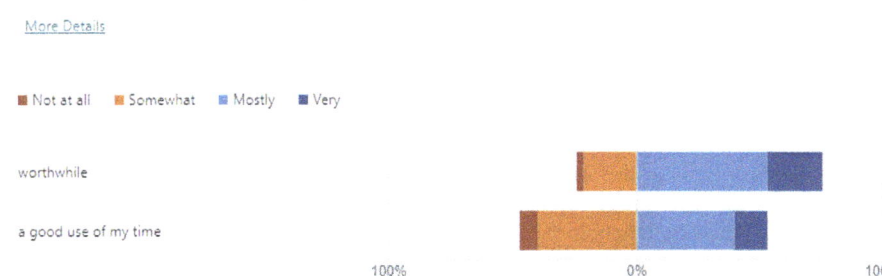

"I think going through the peer review really helps to understand the main learning outcomes from the assessed exersise (sic) so being a marker, I would go through each answer and understand it clearly."

"Autonomy in self-reflection while practicing marking was valuable."

15

ePortfolios go to the Parks: Lessons learned from Honors Immersive Service-Learning and Leadership Academic Programs

Dr. Chelsea Redger-Marquardt, Dr. Kimberly Engber & Aaron Valentine
The Dorothy and Bill Cohen Honors College, Wichita State University, US

The Context

BILL'S Trip (Building Investment in Lifelong Leadership & Service) is a signature experience available to all Cohen Honors College students. The program engages students in contemporary scholarship and relevant applied learning via a service-learning partnership with a National Park Service (NPS) unit. Students collaborate, create a sense of belonging with their team, connect with National Park Rangers, and engage in volunteer work and on-site educational sessions facilitated by NPS leaders and faculty from Wichita State University. The importance of preparing to serve, reflecting, and meaning making is well documented in service-learning and leadership development (Buschlen & Warner, 2014; Niehaus, 2012; Redger-Marquardt & Patterson, 2023; Sumka, Porter, & Piacitelli, 2015).

The program includes a PebblePad Workbook organized into pre/on/post-trip sections. The eportfolio Workbook structures student engagement with the course material and immersive service-learning programming. The pre-and post-trip sections create a common asynchronous space for meaning making. In the on-trip section, the learner is asked to engage in guided reflection, the process of noticing, recording, and reflecting after long, immersive days of service. The Workbook serves as a facilitator of sorts, allowing students the freedom to step away in the evening in a shared living space and register their reactions to the experience. The variety of engagement supports diverse students and enhances group dynamics. Beginning with the pilot and into our third year, the eportfolio has been a lynchpin for BILL'S Trip. From the flexibility of just-in-time support to demonstrating the entire arc of learning for the connected course, the eportfolio allows for reflection, authentic feedback, and a shared space for students to navigate success in the course. This case study is based on observations and feedback from three locations: Chickasaw National Recreation Area, Zion, and Grand Canyon National Park.

2022	2023	2024
Chickasaw National Recreation Area (Oklahoma, United States)	Zion National Park (Utah, United States)	Grand Canyon National Park (Arizona, United States)

The Cohen Honors College has been engaged in eportfolio development at the course level since the spring 2020. Increased engagement, including program-level engagement with all first-year students, began in fall 2022. A multi-college multidisciplinary team also participated in the year-long AAC&U ePortfolio Institute from January 2022-January 2023. This program included work with a faculty mentor, multiple professional development sessions, and collaboration with a campus-based team of faculty engaged with eportfolio development and implementation. As a result of the institute, our college began to explore research opportunities framed with the Scholarship of Teaching Learning (Chick, 2018).

The Problem

BILL'S Trip offered a unique opportunity for our students. The program and course can be defined as activities that occur pre-trip, on-trip, and post-trip. As such the resources provided for students to learn, engage, consider, and reflect needed to be nimble. Further the course spanned traditional academic semesters.

In the first stage (pre-trip), students participate in a pre-trip kick-off meeting during the month of December. Over the winter break, they complete several foundational assignments in preparation for engagement with the NPS park unit. The resources therefore need to be clear, scaffolded, and available to students in an "on-demand" format/environment. Pre-trip assignments are completed prior to the January pre-session travel aspect of the program.

In the second stage (on-trip), students travel to serve and learn in partnership with our NPS unit during the university's January pre-session. As an important aspect of service-learning is reflection and as this course experience is multidisciplinary with outcomes tied to knowledge and action rather than modes of expression, resources provided need to allow students to capture reflective thoughts via narrative and visuals.

Finally, the post-trip stage asks students to continue to make meaning of their experience, apply their learned understanding, and think about continued next steps as a result of this experience. The post-trip assignments are completed after the official January session semester has concluded.

Beyond facilitating the untraditional timing of the course, the resources need to allow students to capture applied learning that happens outside of the four walls of a classroom. They need to be mobile friendly for use during travel and need to be engaging for the student learners.

We wanted students to have a meaningful signature experience and ongoing reflection on their own development. We knew we needed something more dynamic than our Learning Management System. We needed to meet the variety of needs that arise with immersive applied learning. In other words, the course resources needed to mirror in some ways the adaptability we wanted to foster through the educational experience. Our aim was to provide students an integrated textbook, assignment framework, and reflective tool that captured photo, video, narrative, sketches, and mapping. Further, we hoped for something students would use and refer to beyond the time limits of a semester.

The Approach

We created a multi-level PebblePad Workbook to support student learning throughout the entirety of the BILL'S Trip program's connected course. Students were introduced to the PebblePad platform (though some had used PebblePad before in other honors courses) and given access to the course Workbook as part of the December pre-trip meeting.

Pre-Trip Assignments included service-learning modules, indigenous voice podcasts and readings, documentary film clips, NPS stewardship podcasts, poetry and essays, and connection to nature scales that required students to contribute content by recording and uploading sounds from nature.

On-Trip Assignments included a daily reflection journal to record the student experience in multiple media formats.

Post-Trip Assignments included an impact video, leadership profiles, and preparing a presentation for a university level service-learning showcase.

A single Workbook allows for a one-stop home for content, integrative thinking, and reflection activities across the time windows and varied locations that students' experience and learning occurred. This sometimes looks like a traditional student at a desk, or it might look like a student in an outdoor space on their phone or riding in a bus to/from the NPS destination.

The below visual provides an overview of the Workbook ecosystem:

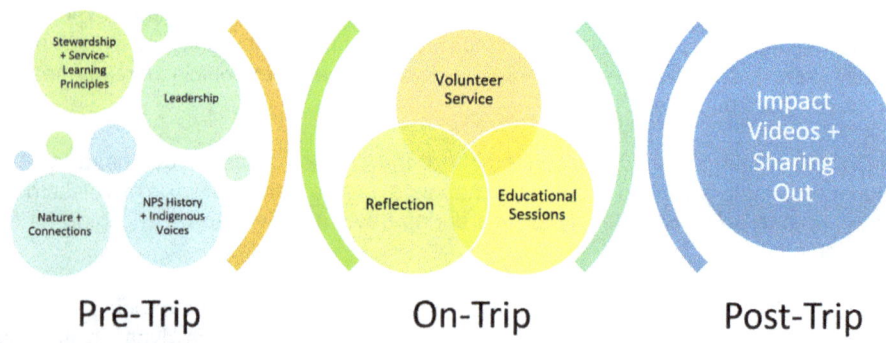

Figure 1: Overview of the BILL's Trip Workbook ecosystem.

The Results and Feedback

Meeting the students where, when, and how they want to learn is possible because of the nimbleness of PebblePad, which guides student learning in the parks and extends beyond the immersive experience through post-trip assignments. Students create impact videos and caption photos with reflective narratives; PebblePad captures each form of expression. Honors is multidisciplinary, and having a tool that allows for creative and critical reflection is vital to capture each student's unique story. Through the PebblePad Workbook students see how their learning is scaffolded and a roadmap to success for the course. It allows students to think in moments of understanding and capture that for further introspection. Co-instructor teams can create a comprehensive curriculum for the annual program.

In the most recent cohort to Grand Canyon National Park, students were asked to give informal feedback responding to questions about how PebblePad supported their learning, what their favorite things are, and what they would change. Below is a summary of their responses including student testimonials.

Support Learning:

- Scaffolding
- Things being in a common place.
- Timing- disparate times being brought together with Workbook
- Tool for applied learning, particularly those activities that are not bounded by the semester
- Intuitive

Student testimonials:

> "It allowed me to change my thoughts as I went along. During pre-trip, I was able to do assignments and save them and come back a couple days later an revisit them and change what I saw. This allowed my learning to continue after seeing something multiple times. It also helped separate what I needed to do so that I did not feel like I had to do everything at once."

> "PebblePad was very easy to learn, and I understood how to do the pre-trip assignments almost immediately. The pre-trip assignments also adequately prepared me for what I would be learning about on the trip. The on-trip assignments were also easy to access, understand, and accomplish. I even work[ed] on some of them while on the bus. These post trip assignments are also overall easy to accomplish."

> "Having all information was very beneficial. Not having any formal class before the trip made the pre-class assignments all the more helpful and it was nice to have all needed information in one place."

Favorite Things:

- All in one place.
- Easy to navigate.
- Ability to attach multimedia, not just narrative.
- Well organized.

"My favorite thing about this space is how organized and user-friendly it is. I often have technical difficulties, but those were minimized with this platform. I really liked how easy it was to read the homework articles, answer the questions, and upload content all in one space."

"The different segments of PebblePad made the layout very easy to understand and digest. It isn't very hard to navigate and you're rarely lost."

Change:

- Auto-save, lack of. (most commonly noted change)
- Text boxes.
- Technical Difficulties. (finding assets, file types being supported, desire for notifications and reminders)
- Instructions and prompts. (a small number of students reported a desire for more robust instructions and less repetitive on-trip reflection prompts)

Student testimonials:

"I always forget to hit the save button so I would say that's my least favorite thing."

"Some of the options for submission areas could be changed, as the text sometimes wanders and it becomes hard to see your entire thought."

"Make it easier to find documents and workbooks. I have spent 20 minutes trying to find a single asset I have had to do that took me 5 minutes."

"Sometimes you will upload an image, but it will not appear. Just takes a little bit more effort."

Lessons Learnt

- Workbook allowed for changes in content/ student support when location/ programmatic changes occurred.
- Workbook allowed for an onboarding reference for new faculty guides during year three of the program.
- Workbook is particularly helpful in creating a learning environment that prepares students to engage in an applied learning experience. Students felt prepared in terms of knowledge and ready to engage with their peers. Allows instructors to bring in a diverse group of students and create a baseline prior to on-trip community forming.
- Students reported ease of use via an asynchronous tool that supported learning especially during pre- and post-trip assignments.
- Next time build a final assignment into the post-trip Workbook that encourages the students to create a showcase eportfolio page featuring their impact video. This would allow for continued cohesion with college level program assessment with Honors Learner Outcomes.

In Brief

- Building content rich, student-centred academic resources can greatly impact student learning, lessen faculty administrative tasks, and enhance collaborative teaching.
- Showing students where you want them to go by scaffolding their learning is powerful. One student shared that their learning could continue throughout the experience and the Workbook allowed the opportunity to revisit assignments as their thoughts developed.
- Students appreciated an integrated resource that captured disparate timeframes of learning.
- Multimedia combined with narrative meets the learners where they are. Students noted they enjoyed using photos and other forms of media to express themselves.

References

Buschlen, E., & Warner, C. (2014). We're not in Kansas anymore. Disaster relief, social change leadership, and transformation. *Journal of Student Affairs Research and Practice, 51(3)*, 311-322. https://doi.org/10.1515/jsarp-2014-0031

Chick, N. (2018). SoTL in action: Illuminating critical moments of practice. Sterling, VA: Stylus Publishing.

Niehaus, E. (2012). *Alternative break programs and the factors that contribute to changes in students' lives.* [Doctoral Dissertation, University of Maryland]. ProQuest Dissertations and Theses Global.

Redger-Marquardt, C., & Patterson, J. A. (2023). Preparing to serve: Sensemaking, sensegiving, and diversity learning in an alternative break program and connected honors course. *Journal of the National Collegiate Honors Council, 24(2)*, 95-121. https://digitalcommons.unl.edu/nchcjournal/773

Sumka, S., Porter, M. C., Williams, T. O., & Piacitelli, J. (2015). Working side by side: Creating alternative creaks as catalysts for global learning, student leadership, and social change. Stylus Publishing.

16

Extending the use of PebblePad to meet Australian Nursing standards and organisational vision through AAA signature pedagogy

Jo-Anne Rihs
Nursing Discipline, Royal Melbourne Institute of Technology, AU

The Context

Nursing curriculums in Australian universities are accredited every 5 years by the national governing body, the Australian Nursing and Midwifery Accreditation Council (ANMAC). In addition, as nursing curriculums, leading to graduates' registration as nurses, are all taught within the Higher Education Tertiary system (universities), the curriculums must also align with the national standards and requirements of the Tertiary Education Quality Assurance and Standards Agency (TEQASA). At the time of accreditation, concepts of learning are developed to align with identified healthcare industry change and need.

In addition to the national levels of governance, each university offering a nursing curriculum has its unique organisational governance. The Royal Melbourne Institute of Technology (RMIT), recognised historically as an applied learning institution, embodies this through its Education Plan, 'Learning through Life and Work,' aligning with the university's signature pedagogy. Lee Shulman's (2005) seminal concept of signature pedagogies emphasises that they "organize the fundamental ways in which future practitioners are educated for their new professions" (p. 52). In essence, signature pedagogies guide students to act, think, and behave in ways that reflect the expectations of qualified practitioners. At RMIT, this signature pedagogy is known as Active, Applied, and Authentic (AAA) learning. 'Active' denotes active engagement in learning, 'Applied' signifies the direct application of skills and knowledge in hands-on and real-world settings, while 'Authentic' fosters an understanding of concepts and practices through the integration of previously learned knowledge and exposure.

Another layer of university oversight involves RMIT Graduate Attributes, representing the identified qualities and skills the institution anticipates students to cultivate, equipping them for lifelong learning, professional practice, and global citizenship. The loop of governance and accreditation is closed through tangible, audited proof that every Australian nursing curriculum meets the Australian Nursing Standards (NMBA) and adheres to the National Safety and Quality Health Service (NSQHS) standards, ensuring the delivery of safe, high-quality care throughout the healthcare system. This not only prioritises patient safety but also establishes accountability to the public and regulatory bodies.

Within the layers of accreditation, governance, standards, and regulations that shape nursing curriculums, the dynamic nature of the healthcare sector necessitates a keen focus on students' learning needs, teaching strategies, and assessment methods.

In this intricate context of curriculum development, characterised by the necessity for agile and nimble responses to changing expectations and advancements, the innovative utilisation of PebblePad was conceived to revitalize both learning and assessment processes.

The Problem

The challenge, simply expressed, was to weave the national and organisational governance and standards requirements in an innovative way to maximise student engagement and learning outcomes grounded in the AAA signature pedagogy and contributing to students meeting the Graduate Attributes. Previously the course design was traditional with a tendency to be linear, which according to Hase (2009) is not dynamic and may hinder the student's ability to effectively engage in learning. Contemporary transformations of nursing curriculums focus on integrating mapping, evaluation, and revision (Aul et al., 2021). Thus, the harnessing of innovation through the use of PebblePad and a single multi-faceted assessment task opens up new and exciting opportunities to fully engage students as active learners.

The students in this case study were second-year undergraduate nursing students who were enrolled in the unit "Therapeutics in Nursing Practice 2" during Semester 1, 2023. This unit is a component of a three-year Bachelor of Nursing program, following foundational first-year units. The "Therapeutics in Nursing Practice 2" unit serves as a bridge between Pharmacology concepts and the practical application of pharmacological knowledge and skills in nursing, emphasising the connection between theory and practice. Considering the unit requirements, accreditation elements, and the critical role of medication safety in patient care, an assessment based on the principles of RMIT signature pedagogy, AAA, was devised, aligning with essential frameworks, standards, and RMIT graduate attributes. The pursuit of authentic learning and assessment practices prompted an exploration and adoption of heutagogy as an underpinning theoretical construct with an understanding of its primary suitability for the Tertiary Education setting and the application of AAA learning. By embracing and applying heutagogy theory, focus shifts to the student with a learner-centred approach emphasising student determination of learning path and assists students to understand how they learn (Blaschke, 2016), providing a framework for students to take ownership of their learning and self-directed, self-determined, and lifelong learning skills that they need to succeed in their chosen field. (Blaschke, 2021).

The Approach

Comprehensive mapping of the whole nursing curriculum was performed at the time of accreditation. A revision of this unit created an updated and comprehensive mapping, aligned with the AAA signature pedagogy, Australian Nursing Standards and Australian NSQHS Standards, unit learning outcomes and graduate attributes. This revision evolved from a mind-map to a tabulated visual identity (See Appendix A). This 'as is' evaluation provided insight into gaps, challenges, and opportunities for improvements.

The layering of heutagogy principles under the unit content and the use of PebblePad was envisioned. This was to facilitate students meeting required learning outcomes and demonstrating their ability to engage their knowledge and skill in regard to medication safety principles and therefore safe patient care. Heutagogy is a beneficial framework for both educators and learners where an active role in learning and the use of technology may drive innovative education (Gerstein 2013). Whilst providing the ability to design learning experiences to suit individual student needs, heutagogy also enables educators to use flexible and adaptable teaching strategies incorporating the use of programs such as PebblePad innovatively and in line with real-world constructs.

The implementation of a digital PebblePad Workbook enabled learner-centred pedagogies, the use of self-efficacy, self-determination, constructivism, self-evaluation, reflection, and self-directed learning, all of which are evident active learning processes. Experiential demonstration of skill brought the students into the applied approach to learning, authenticity focused on the student's ability to provide 'safe patient care'. An added dimension through the use of PebblePad is the use of 'Net-Aware' pedagogies such as complexity, connectivism and rhizomatic learning which intertwine with a heutagogical approach to learning (Blaschke & Hase, 2019) creating transferable digital confidence.

A Workbook comprising four components was developed and implemented via PebblePad. At the commencement of the semester, students were introduced to the Workbook to facilitate their familiarity with the assessment requirements, the PebblePad program, and the PebblePocket mobile application. The individual elements of the Workbook and the associated learning content were synchronised with the course syllabus and learning activities. This alignment allowed students the flexibility to "work ahead" or progress through the Workbook at a pace that suited their individual learning journey at any given stage. The four components that made up the Workbook are explored and mapped in detail in Appendix A, however these signature pedagogy AAA elements included:

- Skill Demonstration and Self-Reflection
- Pharmacology Portfolio Page
- Collection of Artefacts
- Interprofessional Experience (IPE)

PebblePad created the opportunity to challenge traditional and linear course and assessment design via bespoke assessment practical activities following the notion of practical knowledge; enabling students to transfer learning from problem to problem, from action to action, exhibiting their understanding in ways that aligned with their personal learning styles. Students were exposed to diverse and authentic sources of information and expertise with the impact of being active in their learning by challenging their assumptions and perspectives. Encouraged to map their learning to the RMIT graduate attributes, students could discern the transferability of their knowledge and how it contributed to their development as work-ready graduates.

The Results

Shared learning pathways

Unexpectedly, the use of PebblePad created a paradigm of rapport and camaraderie between the coordinator and the students that facilitated simultaneous but separate learning pathways. This arose as initially the students were skeptical of PebblePad, and the course coordinator was unfamiliar with many PebblePad intricacies; learning alongside the students created a sense of shared journeying and learning bond of the tool.

Student outputs varied from interesting to imaginative

Using programs such as PebblePad allows students to take an active role in creation, consumption, and demonstration of their learning and gives rise to flexibility for how and when and where learning occurs (Moore, 2020). The ability for students to 'pace' their completion of each of the four elements of this assessment over the semester enhanced their time management abilities and choices. Student engagement with the Workbook had peaks and troughs representative of assessment commitments as expected. Some students thrived in the opportunity to be creative and display their knowledge and skill accompanied by creative visual components. Others thrived with the organisation and structure of the Workbook and emphasis for these students was on ensuring all criteria for assessment were met with minimal to no 'extra'.

Enhanced student metacognition

One of the goals was to boost student confidence, motivation, and critical thinking skills by providing them with a comprehensive and practical foundation in therapeutic nursing practice. In achieving this goal, the learner's capacity for lifelong learning, adaptability, and innovation mirror the graduate attributes of the university but also the standards of Australian Registered Nurses.

Enhanced student digital literacy skills

Whilst not initially considered an objective or learning outcome for this assessment, developing and implementing the PebblePad Workbook provided the students with a AAA signature pedagogy platform to build on their digital literacy skills. This informal learning inadvertently engaged the student within a context and setting of digital literacy. Digital literacy for healthcare workers is an ever-evolving requirement with the introduction of Electronic Medical Records. It is considered that having adequate digital literacy among nursing students positivity impacts electronic documentation, communication, and collaboration, and harnesses their ability to search for information in line with evidence-based practice (Harerimana, Duma and Mtshali, 2022).

Reduced evaluation time for academic assessors

Effective time management for marking academics was an unexpected yet positive outcome. With assessment policy dictating the length of marking 'turn-around', academic assessors indicated that once they had become familiar with the application of scorecards and feedback within PebblePad the marking appeared more effective and efficient, enabling timely marking completion with the provision of comprehensive feedback for students.

Lessons Learnt

Initial Introduction

It is crucial to introduce students to the platform early in their undergraduate journey through smaller, lightly weighted assessments. This early exposure familiarises students with PebblePad and its functionalities. The lower weighting at the outset allows students to absorb feedback, refining their interaction for subsequent assessments with higher weightings. This approach enhances overall student application and proficiency on the platform.

Sequential Guidance

Provide detailed, step-by-step instructions for locating the assessment in the learning management system, initiating the assessment, and navigating within the platform. Whether in a classroom setting or through a video demonstration, this method enables students to follow along. Having a structured process provides students with a point of reference throughout the development of their assessment submission, ensuring they are accurately navigating the assessment task.

Syllabus alignment

Ensuring alignment with the weekly syllabus, the four Workbook elements are strategically designed for progressive completion. Scaffolding the weekly learning in direct correlation with Workbook elements aids students in managing their time effectively. Furthermore, transparent mapping and alignment with critical frameworks, standards, and attributes immerse students in the nursing culture, fostering continuous development of their nursing identity within the evolving journey from nursing student to registered nurse.

Centring and Recentering

The workbook functioned as the primary evaluation tool within the unit, blending both theoretical and practical demonstration of learning. Strategically guiding student focus as the semester progressed ensured continued and progressive completion towards the due date. This strategic guidance of students at various intervals aimed to maintain momentum and enthusiasm, fostering engagement and connections with learning and nursing culture; whilst offering an extension of support for any students that had 'fallen behind'.

Leveraging on 2023 insights, 2024 second-year nursing students will now use PebblePad and PebblePocket with increased confidence and engagement as they transition from first to second year, fostering creativity, motivation, ownership, and a sense of achievement.

Adapting the curriculum to rejuvenate assessments while adhering to accreditation parameters presents a challenging complexity. The incorporation of AAA learning and assessment opportunities empowers learners to construct knowledge through meaningful connections. Utilising PebblePad, along with associated learning and assessment elements, serves as a powerful tool to showcase tangible examples of learning and growth throughout the entire nursing student journey. This approach seamlessly aligns with pedagogy, learning outcomes, RMIT graduate attributes, NMBA Nursing Standards, NSQHS standards, and fosters transferrable digital confidence, identity, and cultural competence.

In Brief

- Explore initial construct concepts, think non-linear and reimagine.
- Embrace shared learning journeys with students.
- Be open to unexpected outcomes

Feedback

> *"My initial thoughts were positive, I'm a big fan of breaking away from the usual 1500-word academic papers, not that I don't realize their purpose and value but when you have to write 6 of them a semester it gets a bit dry. The workbook being broken up into sections with differing themes and objectives helped me organize and digest the workbook assignment more easily, despite it having a completed wordcount and workload much higher (500 for video reflection and IPE, x4 artefact descriptions and a huge medications portfolio section) than just an average written piece with headings. Digitization is easily a plus, being able to organize and compile our assets into an online storage hub that we can then pull from when working on the objectives is efficient and convenient and reduces accidental deletion or loss if we were just using PC/MAC OS files."*

KC

> *"The interactivity of the app allowed me to design my work with images in a way that I found satisfying. The app also updates me of any feedback added via email, which I appreciated."*

IA

> *"As a student coming from the diploma where we had to print out, fill out, copy, scan and send back work... pebble pad is leaps and bounds beyond paper-based assessments."*

EB

References

Aul, K., Bagnall, L., Bumbach, M. D., Gannon, J., Shipman, S., McDaniel, A., & Keenan, G. (2021). A key to transforming a nursing curriculum: Integrating a continuous improvement simulation expansion strategy. *SAGE Open Nursing, 7*, 1-7. https://doi.org/10.1177/2377960821998524

Blaschke, L.M. (2016). Self-Determined Learning: Designing for Heutagogic Learning Environments. In: Spector, M., Lockee, B., Childress, M. (eds) *Learning, Design, and Technology*. Springer, Cham. https://doi.org/10.1007/978-3-319-17727-4_62-1

Blaschke, L. M. (2021). The dynamic mix of Heutagogy and technology: Preparing learners for lifelong learning. *British Journal of Educational Technology, 52(4)*, 1629–1645. https://doi.org/10.1111/bjet.13105

Blaschke, L.M. and Hase, S. (2019). Heutagogy and digital media networks: Setting students on the path to lifelong learning. *Pacific Journal of Technology Enhanced Learning, 1(1)*, 1-14. https://doi.org/10.24135/pjtel.v1i1.1

Gerstein, J. (2013. Education 3.0 and the Pedagogy (Andragogy, Heutagogy) of Mobile Learning. Retrieved from https://usergeneratededucation.wordpress.com/2013/05/13/education-3-0-and-the-pedagogy-andragogy-heutagogy-of-mobile-learning/

Harerimana, A., Duma, S.E, and Mtshali, N.G (2022), First-year nursing students' digital literacy: A cross-sectional study. *Journal of Nursing Education and Practice, 13(1)*, 31 – 37. https://doi.org/10.5430/jnep.v13n1p31

Hase, S. (2009). Heutagogy and e-learning in the workplace: Some challenges and opportunities. *Impact: Journal of Applied Research in Workplace E-learning, 1(1)*, 43-52.

Moore, R.L. (2020). Developing lifelong learning with heutagogy: contexts, critiques, and challenges. *Distance Education, 41(3)*, 381-401. https://doi.org/10.1080/01587919.2020.1766949

Shulman, L. S. (2005). Signature pedagogies in the professions. *Daedalus, 134(3)*, 52-59. https://doi.org/10.1162/0011526054622015

Appendix A: Mapping the Therapeutics in Nursing 2 Workbook Assessment to RMIT signature pedagogy, Australian Nursing Standards for Practice and National Safety and Quality Health Service (NSQHS) Standards

Authentic	Active and Applied	Nursing Standards*	NSQHS Standards**
Element 1: Skill Demonstration and Self-Reflection	Students used the PebblePocket App to record their Intramuscular (IM) Injection preparation and administration, adhering to safe medication principles. The video was not competency based; instead, students self-evaluated using a checklist and wrote reflections using the DIEP template. Reflections included reviewing NMBA Nursing standards and noting links to relevant nursing legislation.	1.1, 1.2, 1.4, 3.3, 3.4, 3.5, 3.6, 4.1, 4.4, 5.1, 5.3, 5.5, 6.1, 6.2, 6.5, 7.1, 7.2, 7.3	Clinical Governance Preventing and Controlling Infection Comprehensive Care Medication Safety
Element 2: Pharmacology Portfolio	Students created a Pharmacology portfolio page in PebblePad, showcasing their ability to connect theory to practice for four medications. Drawing on the syllabus, which covered clinically used medications through case studies and labs, students had creative freedom to demonstrate learning. The portfolio included essential elements like pharmacokinetics, pharmacodynamics, and nursing considerations.	1.1, 3.2, 3.3, 3.7, 4.3, 4.4, 6.1	Comprehensive Care Medication Safety Partnering with consumers

Authentic	Active and Applied	Nursing Standards*	NSQHS Standards**
Element 3: Collection of Artefacts	Students connected theory to practice by identifying artefacts related to safe patient care, including medication safety policies, procedures, standards, and practices. They sourced diverse artefacts aligning with safe medication principles, briefly justifying their choices for importance, and indicating links to the National Safety and Quality Healthcare Service (NSQHS) standards.	1.1, 1.2, 1.7, 3.3, 3.5, 3.6, 3.7, 4.3, 4.4	Clinical Governance Medication Safety
Element 4: Prprofessional Experience (IPE)	Nursing and Pharmacy students collaborated in nursing labs to review medication charts and treatment options for simulated patient case studies. The interdisciplinary teamwork focused on exploring changes to patient care through pharmacological orders and interventions. Nursing students demonstrated clinical reasoning based on the critical thinking of Pharmacy students regarding prescribed medications. Through reflective practice, students addressed the question "Why is interdisciplinary collaboration important for safe patient care standards?" using a provided template, with a focus on reviewing and linking to NMBA nursing standards.	1.1, 1.2, 1.4, 1.5, 1.7, 2.2, 2.6, 2.7, 2.8, 3.3, 3.5, 3.6, 4.3, 4.4, 5.1, 5.2, 6.1, 6.2, 6.5, 7.3	Clinical Governance Comprehensive Care Medication Safety Communicating for Safety Standard

*The full list and description of each Australian Nursing Standards can be found at Nursing and Midwifery Board of Australia - Registered nurse standards for practice (nursingmidwiferyboard.gov.au)

**The full list and description of the National Safety and Quality Health Service (NQSHS) Standards can be found at Australian Commission on Safety and Quality in Health Care - The NSQHS Standards

17

Transforming a student placement portfolio: A seven-year evolution towards personalised learning and success

Rebecca Scriven[1] & Brooke Chapman[2]
[1]Centre for Learning and Teaching, Edith Cowan University, AU
[2]School of Arts & Humanities, Edith Cowan University, AU

The Context

At the end of a three-year course of study in the Bachelor of Social Science at Edith Cowan University (ECU) students complete a year-long capstone unit which includes 400 hours of professional placement in various community and service agencies. The unit includes some class attendance time at the start of the year, and long periods of time where students are not attending class while they are attending placements. Prior to 2017, students recorded their placement details in a paper-based portfolio and submitted their work in the final week of their unit. For assurance of learning, students provide evidence of their meeting accreditation requirements with the Australian Community Workers Association (ACWA) Practice Guidelines (ACWA, 2021). The guidelines provide a framework for community work practice and are relevant to students for preparing them for future work practice. The students provide three pieces of evidence and three reflections for each of the eight guidelines. Unit learning outcomes are focused on developing a portfolio of knowledge and skills to meet practice guidelines and the demonstration of the implementation of the knowledge of skills during the practicum. Students provide evidence of the integration of theoretical learning and practical application during their practicums, across a range of contexts. While on practicum students are supervised by the placement agency and have contact with their Unit Coordinator (UC) and ECU practicum supervisor. As a capstone unit, much of the preparation for employment is covered as part of the unit content and students are required to submit their CV as part of the final portfolio assessment.

This case study examines the approach taken to convert the paper-based portfolio to a digital portfolio to monitor student progression and its development and improvements over the last seven years. The design of the portfolio has seen improved feedback mechanisms, record keeping and support, particularly for online students, resulting in improved satisfaction and success rates. The portfolio has become an invaluable resource for both the unit coordinator and students alike.

The Problem

Using a paper-based portfolio presented several challenges for the UC. It was difficult to establish a connection with her students and monitor their progress, making it hard to provide the appropriate support. With only one point of assessment, there was no way to provide feedback throughout the year, and the UC reported a wide variation in the quality of the work submitted. Once physical portfolios were submitted, there was no opportunity for reflection, as students completed their assessment and did not revisit their portfolio again. The progress of students studying online was even more indefinable with many not in regular contact with the UC or fellow students. Mentoring and advice provided while on placement can be a powerful influence on student employability (Oliver, 2021). Without regular contact with students, it was difficult to provide advice until planned supervision meetings were arranged. In a capstone unit, this assessment provides an opportunity to offer advice and mentoring regarding their professional practice, which is crucial to student success.

ECU has been awarded a 5-star rating for undergraduate teaching quality for the past 17 years, and highly values the student experience, placing high quality learning experiences and student support at the forefront of their strategic objectives. Monitoring student learning at key points in the semester, and providing feedback and support are essential to promoting student learning and success (Brown & Race, 2021). The move to a digital portfolio has enabled the UC to monitor student progression throughout the year and provide timely feedback and support.

Over the seven years of the portfolio development, the UC and the Senior Learning Designer (SLD) have adapted the instructions and support materials for students. Originally an in-class demonstration and learning activity were used to introduce students to the portfolio. As support roles and availability changed, the support materials have become more self-directed, with recordings and documents provided for students to access as needed. Targeted support for the portfolio assessment has been an issue over the seven years, with general IT support and peer student support available from the institution to assist students with the basics of logging in, editing and accessing their work. However, the UC and SLD consistently provide support for more detailed issues with the portfolio itself. This has proved challenging and yearly reviews and updates to support materials have not solved the support issue. Feedback from students around the use of PebblePad has not always been favourable and it has been difficult to determine why the value of the portfolio is not recognised by students.

The Approach

In 2016, working closely with the UC, the SLD began to develop a workbook and portfolio, based on the paper-based portfolio. To introduce the UC to PebblePad and ATLAS, a workbook was created based on the Career Development Learning exercises the students were previously completing and submitting in document format. The UC began to see the students' progression through this workbook and was easily able to mark the work online. After this experience, the UC became keen to introduce the full Professional Placement Portfolio for 2017.

The portfolio design was created with three objectives in mind:

- To enable the UC to establish a rapport with students and monitor their progress.
- To provide necessary documentation for placement.
- To encourage students to reflect on their experience and learning.

Early discussions determined that a portfolio rather than a workbook would allow students to add their own personal elements and customisations. This was an important factor for the UC, allowing her to get to know the students and foster connections. An 'About Me' page was added as a starting point, allowing the students to introduce themselves and write about their interests and goals. It doubled as an introduction to the PebblePad resource and was used in class to demonstrate PebblePad and how to edit, customise and add page elements. The 'About Me' me page has remained over the seven years as an invaluable tool for both the students and the UC. It gives the UC her first introduction to the student with the addition of a photo allowing her to connect names and faces, and the paragraph written by the student give insight into their interests and personality, and also their reflective writing abilities.

Students receive a portfolio template at the beginning of the year and once automatically submitted, begin adding their own elements as well as completing the required workbook sections as their placements occur. A mid-year portfolio review was incorporated to allow the UC to review the student's progress midway through the unit and provide feedback on their progress. Feedback was originally added into an assessor field as part of the mid-year review page but has now progressed to include a feedback form with comments left throughout the portfolio and collected via the feedback panel. This has allowed for a richer, deeper form of targeted feedback and allows the students to easily locate where more attention is needed in their portfolio.

University placement documentation requirements around risk management and insurance determined the contents of the placement workbooks. A pre and post placement workbook was designed to record what was needed for each placement, and if required, more placement workbooks could be easily added to the portfolio. Over the seven years, the amount of documentation required in the portfolio has been reduced as the University has shifted to using other placement recording software. Students are now required to upload documentation to these systems, and sometimes to their portfolio as well. A placement manual has been developed including instructions and forms to ensure students know where and what to upload.

A reflective journal was added to allow students to easily record their experiences while on placement. Students are required to write a minimum of twenty reflections, focussing on their development as a student, graduate and future professional. The reflective journal has become an invaluable tool for fostering connections between the UC and students. The reflective journal provides insight into the student's wellbeing during placement and serves as a trigger for the UC to contact the student offering extra support or advice, and sometimes debrief and offer referral to further support services if required.

At the end of each placement workbook a 'Reflection and Review' section allows students to reflect on their learning during placement and the integration of their classroom learning into the professional placement. Students are asked to reflect on the challenges faced during placement and identify further skills they may need to develop.

The Results

The original goal of moving to a digital portfolio to monitor student progression was immediately achieved, and the UC was extremely happy with the ability to view students' progress at any time during the year. Over the seven years, other benefits have emerged that were not expected. The portfolio has promoted connections between the UC and students, and student engagement and progress has been easily monitored throughout the unit. The reflective blog informs the UC of any issues that may need to be addressed by contacting the student. Early in the unit the UC can easily see which students are struggling to articulate their learning experiences and provide guidance and learning support. To meet the accreditation requirements, it is essential that students provide sufficient evidence and reflection on their experiences, in accordance with the ACWA practice guidelines. The UC can now identify students who are struggling to meet these requirements and guide them towards improvement. By providing the opportunity for reflection on their developing skills, students have gained insight into their professional practice, noting that the journals have helped them make the link between theory and practice.

Another unexpected benefit has been the ability to assess the placement agencies and their capacity to provide students with the learning opportunities needed. The reflective blog and placement workbooks have provided insight into the agencies themselves, and the UC can determine which agency may suit which student in subsequent years, as she becomes familiar with both the agencies from previous years, and the new students.

There has been an increase in satisfaction with the UC based on student survey feedback from 2019 to 2023, with an increase of 46%. Feedback responses indicate students have found the UCs support to be one of the best aspects of the unit with comments directly mentioning the support and encouragement received.

Although the institution's unit feedback survey does not include direct questions about PebblePad, some students have mentioned it in the 'suggested changes for the unit' section. When reviewing these comments, it is evident that earlier comments from the first years of the digital portfolio focused on the system itself, with some students reporting issues such as lost work or confusion around the use of PebblePad. In later years, comments tended to centre around the assessment requirements, such as, the number of reflections or evidence pieces needed, and suggestions for improved instructions. One aspect of confusion for students that has persisted over the seven years has been around the process of adding evidence to their portfolio. Some students do not understand the difference between uploading evidence pieces to their PebblePad account and adding those pieces to their portfolio for viewing and assessing.

It has become apparent to the UC that there are record keeping aspects of the portfolio that may need to be improved, to ensure students are meeting the accreditation requirements. These will be addressed in future versions. The digital portfolio has allowed long standing records to be reviewed when students contact the UC requiring evidence of their placements for their own accreditation with ACWA, for example when applying for future roles. Being able to easily look back through the last seven years of portfolio submissions for this evidence has been another advantage gained.

Lessons Learnt

PebblePad has provided more benefits than the portfolio was originally designed for. Since moving her assessment online, the UC has never looked back. The student experience has improved with better engagement and communication, and the quality of work submitted has improved, due to the new feedback cycle in place.

Student support, both technological and pedagogical, is essential to enable students to grasp the concept of a portfolio in PebblePad. After reviewing feedback from students over the last seven years, the Learning Designer and UC agree that more information and clarity about the reasons for completing the portfolio are required, as well as the benefits for students related to their future practice. The UC has seen students have genuine 'aha' moments when they understand the link between what they are doing as part of the assessment and the 'why' they are doing it for their professional practice.

Supporting students in the use of PebblePad has proved challenging over the years, with some students understanding it immediately and others struggling. The UC and SLD plan to continue with more research into the reasons behind this anomaly. Surveying the students on their use of the support materials may help pinpoint another area for improvement.

Yearly reviews of the portfolio and implementation of design improvements based on student feedback has contributed to the success of the assessment.

In Brief

- Using a digital placement portfolio has provided an excellent opportunity for the monitoring of student progress throughout placement and for the delivery of timely feedback and learning support to students.
- Regular review and improvements made based on student feedback can lead to bonus outcomes for both the student and teacher experience.
- Providing opportunities for reflections can help guide students towards making the connections between learning theory and practice.

Feedback

The following student feedback comment confirmed our goal of assisting students to make the connections between theory and practice through reflection:

> *"Loved being able to put theoretical learning into practice but then show how practical learning was demonstrated".*

While reflecting on the past seven years of portfolio assessment, the UC commented that she could not return to her previous system. PebblePad has become an essential 'bridge' between university and placement requirements for her students and has provided an opportunity for connection between her students for herself also.

References

Australian Community Workers Association (ACWA). (2021). Australian Community Work Practice Guidelines. Retrieved from https://www.acwa.org.au/wp-content/uploads/2021/08/ACWA-Practice-Guidelines-Aug-2021.pdf

Brown, S. & Race, P. (2021). Using Effective Assessment and Feedback to Promote Learning. In L. Hunt & D. Chalmers (Eds.), *University Teaching in Focus: A Learning-centred* (2 ed., pp. 135-162). Routledge. https://doi.org/10.4324/9781003008330

Oliver, B. (2021). Teaching to Promote Graduate Employability. In L. Hunt & D. Chalmers (Eds.), *University Teaching in Focus: A Learning-centred* (2 ed., pp. 201-216). Routledge. https://doi.org/10.4324/9781003008330

18

Redefining success: PebblePad's journey to reputation recovery

Joseph Spink & David Price
The Higher Education Futures Institute, University of Birmingham, UK

The Context

The Higher Education Futures Institute (HEFi) is an educational support unit that works within the University of Birmingham. HEFi Digital (one half of the department) have a focus on supporting academics in the use of the institution's core digital tools.

This case study will explore HEFi's involvement in;

- The roll out of PebblePad as a tool for Personal Academic Tutoring.
- The initial approach taken.
- Mistakes made along the way.
- Lessons learned.
- Work being done to repair the tool's reputation among academics.

The Problem

The University of Birmingham attempted an institution wide rollout of PebblePad with the intention of having it function as it's Personal Academic Tutoring tool. The speed and scale of this approach led to several complications which, ultimately, resulted in PebblePad being dropped as the preferred Personal Academic Tutoring option. This led to academics losing faith in PebblePad as a tool. We needed to identify ways to re-establish the brand and reputation of PebblePad across the university.

The Approach

In 2017 a working group at the University of Birmingham identified a need for a portfolio platform to support Personal Academic Tutoring, with the aim to drive consistency and engagement across the university. Following a lengthy tender process and contract negotiations, PebblePad was introduced to UoB in July 2018.

After the gathering of initial requirements, a Personal Academic Tutoring workbook was developed. Initially the plan was to roll out the workbook to 1st year undergraduate (UG) students as a pilot across 5 colleges. The process would then be reviewed and improved prior to rolling it out for more students the following year, including postgraduate (PG).

However, it was very quickly decided that it would be rolled out for all students (approximately 39,000 students across UG and PG) by September/October of 2018, which gave us just 3 months to:

- Build the tool, based on the requirements provided by 1 of the 5 colleges.
- Deliver training to academic staff via drop-in sessions and demonstrations.
- Develop staff guidance and online FAQ's for use of the tool.
- Develop resources to support students.
- Create the related VLE course to support the process for each Programme/Year.
- Enroll students.

This was a massive undertaking and many academic staff involved in Personal Academic Tutoring responded negatively to this approach, even before engaging with the Personal Academic Tutoring workbook on PebblePad. This resulted in PebblePad being seen as the Personal Academic Tutoring tool, rather than a broader eportfolio/elearning platform that could support many teaching and learning approaches through customizable workbooks.

The university persevered with the Personal Academic Tutoring workbook in PebblePad, with a range of local customizations employed by schools and PG courses. However, over the past two years many other approaches to Personal Academic Tutoring have been discussed and adopted across much of the University, resulting in the removal of the PebblePad workbook as the core tool.

Reflecting on the Personal Academic Tutoring experience and reviewing feedback received from stakeholders and through user group sessions we identified the following key learnings:

- The importance of early stakeholder engagement in working groups, workshops and training sessions with ample opportunities for feedback.
- The value of running pilots to inform and direct project development and design, and to help plan for the deployment of new solutions.
- While the gathering of requirements is essential for the project to succeed, a one-size fits-all approach can be impractical and may be impossible, especially when dealing with such a complex spread of requirements across an entire University.
- The scale of support required for an institutional rollout cannot be estimated without a meaningful pilot, and exploration of local practice employed across teams who may have additional requirements.

Any future plans to rollout institutionally available workbooks will begin with consultations with working groups to explore requirements and understand how the PebblePad architecture can best support those requirements. A user and pedagogy-first approach will be employed rather than a tool-first approach, and prototypes will be developed as part of a pilot project to evaluate success and identify required tweaks and/or redesign.

Our attention now turns to re-establishing the brand and reputation of PebblePad as a broader eportfolio/elearning tool. By scaling up our support provision, developing a series of eportfolio focused workshops, and ensuring our academics are supported in the implementation of PebblePad, we highlight and share success stories from across the institution and have future plans for further rollouts including;

- The investigation of a staff PDR and CPD record workbook to support staff professional development pathways.
- Using PebblePad as an assessment tool
- Personal portfolio development for both staff and students
- Onboarding activities for students coming to the University

The Results

The process of re-embedding PebblePad institutionally along with reestablishing PebblePad as a platform rather than it being seen as the 'Personal Academic Tutoring' tool is an ongoing challenge. Anecdotally academics who have chosen to revisit PebblePad have commented on their apprehension coming into the project and their relief at how, when used for its intended purposes, PebblePad can provide a beneficial, scaffolded student experience. A number of the success stories are emerging:

- **Inspired@Birmingham**

  This programme supports Year 12 students across the West Midlands who are unsure of what degree they would like to study or what career path they want to pursue. The PebblePad workbook is designed to work alongside a Canvas course and gives the students several short activities (covering topics such as reflection, student life, and choosing a university) that help them to make an informed decision about what they want to study if they choose to join us. It is not submitted to a workspace, but is intended to help the prospective students know what to discuss in the 1 to 1 session they have with their mentors. The Workbook includes a checklist of activities offered through the Inspired@Birmingham programme as well as a notes tab to help scaffold the student's thoughts.

- **Birmingham's Apprenticeship Provision**

  With the need for students, employers, and tutors to be able to access and edit the same resource, PebblePad felt a natural fit for the institution's apprenticeship provision. Utilizing assessor fields, the workbook allows all 3 parties to collectively comment on the apprentice's progress through a Progress Review workbook. This sits within a broader "Apprenticeship Competencies" workbook which asks the student to evidence competencies using PebblePad mapping, log their off the job hours using activity logs, and track their progress through end point assessment rubrics. The administration team leverage the powerful reporting tools within ATLAS to monitor the development and engagement of the hundreds of apprentices across more than 15 offered programmes.

Other ongoing success stories from across the institution include:

- Pharmacy student reflective portfolios used in their living professional portfolio.
- Continued use of Personal Academic Tutoring in PebblePad in some schools.

Lessons Learnt

A barrier was created when PebblePad was initially employed as the Personal Academic Tutoring tool which has caused a reluctance by academics to engage with PebblePad as a tool for other projects and workbooks. Much of this was caused by the rapid implementation of PebblePad as the Personal Academic Tutoring tool. It has been challenging breaking this association with Personal Academic Tutoring and reframing PebblePad as an application which can support many different teaching and learning activities for both staff and students.

Though we have mentioned mainly the impact on academic colleagues, the roll out at scale put many demands on our professional services administrative colleagues which in turn led to some of the problems with the roll out for Personal Academic Tutoring. Re-engaging with administrative teams has also been an essential part of the process and has taught us much about the way tools like this affect process across the digital learning landscape.

It has taken many attempts and offers of engagement with colleagues to determine the best method for re-introducing PebblePad as a possible solution. Much of the process involved us engaging in open and honest conversations around its initial implementation and what we had learned from that.

We also learnt a valuable lesson in when not to recommend PebblePad as a tool. The instinct when trying to revitalise its use was to push it hard, but understanding that PebblePad is a tool with a specific use case meant we were able to set realistic expectations as we focus on suggesting and developing it for suitable projects.

In Brief

- Implementation is everything - no matter how good a tool is, if the process of rolling it out isn't carefully considered the implications can be dire.
- Early stakeholder engagement is essential for the success of a project like this to drive adoption and ownership by staff and students.
- Pedagogy first – you should have a clear idea of what you are trying to assess or teach before considering tools. Bending a solution to fit the needs of a task leads to frustrations around shortcomings.
- Honesty is the first step – being open and honest around the initial implementation and the problems faced led to the rebuilding of academic trust and meant we were able to recommend PebblePad as a solution without it being tarnished with the ghost of Personal Academic Tutoring.

19

Folio Thinking: Teaching to a different test

Sonja Taylor
University Studies, Portland State University, US

The Context

This case study takes place in a dual credit class that is a partnership between Reynolds High School in Troutdale Oregon and Portland State University (PSU) in Portland Oregon. The class is called Power & Imagination, and it is a year-long interdisciplinary college seminar that is co-taught by two high school teachers and one college professor. Students earn required credit for high school as well as 15 college credits from PSU.

The Problem

Since the implementation of the general education program at Portland State, folio thinking and portfolios have been used for assessment related to the learning goals of the general education program, University Studies (UNST). Faculty who designed the program relied on the deep learning and metacognition that is facilitated through the folio thinking process and when technology became available, PSU switched to eportfolios as a mechanism for implementing the portfolio assignment. The greatest benefits of using eportfolio and folio thinking come from embedding folio thinking pedagogy within the courses that use eportfolio assignments. Unfortunately, that piece is often missing in the implementation for a variety of reasons, including lack of professional development related to both pedagogy and practice with our current platform.

As a longtime practitioner of folio thinking and eportfolio, I have worked hard over the years to integrate the eportfolio process more deeply within the activities and assignments in the classrooms where I teach. I was motivated by the desire to make assignments more meaningful, and to help students feel that they did not have a bunch of work tacked on at the end, but to instead experience true folio thinking, a process of organizing and reflecting on work they had already done. I wanted students to reflect in the moment, but also to have an opportunity to see their previous reflections with new eyes at the end of the year. I also wanted students to be able to tell a cohesive story about their learning in Senior Inquiry. Importantly, I wanted them to have an artifact at the end of the year that would be useful for them going forward.

At the same time, I have come to recognize that the practice of folio thinking and the use of eportfolio as a platform for both practicing and showcasing learning is somewhat subversive. Increasingly public education, especially k-12 education, has relied on a practice of standardized testing as a mechanism for measuring student success (Rezai-Rashti & Segeren, 2023; McCarthy & Blake 2017; David, 2011; Posner 2004). Rezai-Rashti and Segeren (2023) argue that high stakes testing in schools was one consequence of the neoliberal shift of the 1980s. As a result, classroom practices have increasingly moved toward teaching to these "high stakes" tests, relying on banking forms of education and assuming a deficit model of thinking in their students. McCarthy & Blake (2017) suggest that such reliance on standardized tests has decreased creativity and is out of step with current needs of our students and society. In contrast, folio thinking (Suter, N.D.) and eportfolio learning provides a space for students to integrate their learning and their life experiences with no preconceived "right" answers and with an emphasis on growth, reflection, and metacognition - all elements of deep learning.

Because of the lack of real learning evidence in practices that involve "teaching to a test", I have been dismissive of the concept and rejected the framework as a means of thinking about teaching and learning. However, in refining my eportfolio scaffolded assignments, I have begun to realize that when I work with students on folio thinking, I am actually teaching to a test, but the test is really student centered and focused on personalized learning that is meaningful for the students who engage in the process.

The Approach

My first iteration of this journey was to design a template for eportfolio with tabs connected to the different UNST goals: Communication; Critical Thinking & Inquiry; Diversity, Equity & Social Justice; Ethics, Agency & Community. While this was helpful for students in organizing their learning, it felt a bit disconnected because it came at the end of the year, and they were stressed out about getting things finished. After my first attempt, I focused on building aspects of the eportfolio throughout the year, but these elements felt disconnected from their daily work in the class and did not tell a cohesive story. One thing that was successful in this attempt was a mapping of digital identity and connecting folio thinking to social media use, but I wasn't where I wanted to be with having students feel that the eportfolio process was deeply connected with all aspects of the course.

In 2017 I started collaborating with a colleague at PSU who works in the Office of Academic Innovation (OAI), Kari Goin Kono, and together we built a series of PebblePad Workbooks that were scaffolded across the year and connected to themes from the Kellog Foundation's guide for truth and racial healing (WK Kellog Foundation, 2016). Our collaboration was published in the Northwest Journal of Teaching (Goin Kono & Taylor, 2022) and I was beginning to see elements of students telling their own story of their learning journey. Building on what I perceived to be the success of the Workbooks focused on academic identity, I built another Workbook for the undergraduate research projects that my students are assigned. This was my first attempt to embed a specific assignment in an eportfolio Workbook and the results were powerful. The process really helped students organize, guide and talk about their work and in 2023 I published an article with four of my students (Taylor, et al., 2023). Our article described the process of combining the high impact practices of writing, research and eportfolio, and was meant as a "how to" for educators interested in following our example.

Through these different iterations I began to see that the more I could integrate assignments in a folio thinking artifact through PebblePad, the more useful it was for my students. Not only did they have a deeper awareness of their learning, but they also had concrete artifacts to share with others and (probably most importantly for them) they did not feel rushed at the end of the year putting their eportfolio together. This year I have pushed even more to figure out how to embed more assignments in a folio thinking process. I have broken out the prompts for Workbooks by typing them out on google docs and printing them out. I then had students give feedback on the prompts and generate ideas for revisions and additions to them. I have looked for ways that students could use assignments already completed to answer sections of the Workbooks they are assigned, and I have created new templates specific to assignment arcs that have illuminated new connections for me, transforming the way I talk about these assignments with my students.

In the remainder of this section, I will focus on two examples that demonstrate my efforts related to using folio thinking and PebblePad to merge eportfolio pedagogy with my regular classroom practices. The first example is creating space for students to choose between three different assignments and copy and paste their finished work in order to satisfy a Workbook prompt. The second example is a completely new template/Workbook that I developed around an assignment arc focused on "Slow Looking".

At the beginning of the year students complete an "Explore Workbook" that gives them a space to introduce themselves and talk about where they are coming from or share their worldview. Additionally, this Workbook provides space for them to reflect on becoming a college student and specifically share photos and reflections from visiting PSU main campus for the first time as a class. The final tab of the Workbook has students connect their initial learning in our course with the four UNST goals. One of the questions on the first tab where students talk about themselves has a prompt that says, "share something about you that you wish everyone knew" and in this space I asked students to choose between three different assignments where they develop and talk about their worldview. The first option was a "for my people" poem that gives students a chance to talk about where they come from and how much their community means to them. The second option was a positionality statement related to their research preparation, in which they talked about aspects of their background that shape their worldview. The final option was a reflection on an "ideological survey" that they took, where the results showed them how they leaned on various ideological axis. The resulting finished product when using these assignments showed a significant shift from how students had answered the prompt previously. It was personal and it told a story, and it connected to their classroom learning. It also made the assignments more relevant and meaningful.

My second example is an assignment arc that combines a visit to an art museum at PSU and the scaffolding of our research project. In order to get ready to do research projects this year, I had students work as a class to develop a community research survey to learn more about the community that we live in. Students developed and revised questions, and then we sent the survey out through various social media and classroom avenues. As a class we interpreted the results as a way to practice data analysis for their individual research projects. Prior to looking at the results of the survey, I had students read an article about "slow looking" that would prepare them for both looking at data and looking at art later in the week.

The slow looking article is academic and quite dense, so I had students "jigsaw" and read the article in class. I read the introduction out loud, and then divided the sections between groups to read and share out to the larger class their takeaways from each section. I then read the conclusion. Slow looking is one practice of many that has arisen as an antidote to the fast-paced world we currently live in. Beene & Thompson (2022) suggest that by slowing down and focusing with intention on the information we are receiving, we can better discern the legitimacy that information. This is particularly important when there is so much misinformation and disinformation inundating our daily lives. Specifically, these authors detail the practice of slow looking when it comes to visual stimuli or artwork. The exercises described in the article to help gain practice with slow looking are meant to "empower learners through intentional dialogue, placing learners' experience at the center of the discussion" (Beene & Thompson, 2022, pg. 3). In this way, slow looking can be connected with the pedagogical influence of Paulo Freire's (1968) "problem-posing" education and could be described as a rejection of the "banking" form of education (Beene & Thompson, 2022, pg. 4).

Mechanically, slow looking involves taking time to notice what is contained within an artifact or a piece of art. One way that students could engage in slow looking is to follow these steps (Beene & Thompson, 2022, pg. 7):

1. Look at an image or object slowly for at least 30 seconds. Let your eyes wander.
2. List 10 words or phrases about anything you notice.
3. Repeat steps 1 & 2, look again, and add 10 more words or phrases about anything you notice.

As the authors note, this strategy is more about describing, rather than categorizing, and they do offer some different strategies to think about throughout the article.

In the next class I had students use some of the techniques and questions from the Slow Looking article to look at the results for 1-2 of the questions from our community survey. I am constantly looking for activities that can serve multiple purposes and I wanted students to practice the slow looking techniques in preparation for the art museum visit the next day as much as I wanted them to use those methods to perform a deeper analysis of the data from our survey. It was a huge success. One of the theories underpinning slow looking techniques is the Aesthetic Development Theory that outlines developmental phases of aesthetic appreciation (Beene & Thompson, 2022). These five stages move from "Accountive" where students make lists of what they see, through Constructive, Classifying, and Interpretive stages to end at the Re-Creative stage (Beene & Thompson, 2022, pg. 5). In the Re-Creative stage students engage with a responsive attitude and several of the groups showed high level interpretation of the community survey data in their reflections and analysis.

I had developed a reflective assignment with the curator of the art museum at PSU and on the way to campus students were given the assignment to look at. When we were taken on a tour of the museum, the tour guide who had developed the assignment with me kept remarking how impressed she was with the students' observations and questions. We took a lot of photos of the different exhibits, and I took several photos of the students engaged in community together. I later put all the photos that I took into a collection in PebblePad to share back with students for anyone who was absent and to supplement the photos each individual student had taken. All these activities culminated in a Workbook/template with two tabs that I developed for students based on the assignment for viewing the art and reading the article on slow looking.

The Results

In building the slow looking Workbook I discovered that I had not only created a sequenced, scaffolded assignment module for embedding eportfolio in everyday classroom learning, but that I had created a template for sharing the assignment, as well as a template for adapting the assignment for future exhibits and for different assignments. My colleague and thought partner in developing the reflective worksheet asked for a report on the assignment to share back with her unit and when she got the report I put together (https://bit.ly/sonja-taylor-report), including student examples, she emailed me saying, "I wish you could see the smile on my face as I read these!!"

Lessons Learnt

Developing this assignment solidified my view that embedding eportfolio in daily classroom experience is a form of "teaching to the test" that we need to explore more broadly. Unlike other forms of structuring coursework so that students get the answers right, in embedded eportfolio learning the test is metacognition and the answer is uniquely individual to each student. Even so, the implications of mastery have a social impact.

In Brief

- Develop assignments with an intention of creating resources for eportfolio work.
- Make specific reflection modules for key assignments.
- Ask students to create a "Digital Learning archive".

Feedback

- Students are encouraged by embedding eportfolio in a way that is relevant to them, and they appreciate the opportunity to go deeper with their learning.
- Colleagues are enthusiastic and want to continue or begin collaborating with me to customize portfolio templates for their own curriculum.

References

Beene, S., & Statton Thompson, D. (2022). Focusing on Slow Looking: An Exploration of Techniques to Develop Critical Observation Habits. Art Documentation: *Journal of the Art Libraries Society of North America, 41(1)*, 1-18.

David, J. L. (2011). Research Says.../High-Stakes Testing Narrows the Curriculum. *Educational Leadership, 68(6)*, 78-80.

Freire, P. (2020). Pedagogy of the oppressed. In *Toward a sociology of education* (pp. 374-386). Routledge.

Goin Kono, K., & Taylor, S. (2022). Leveraging storytelling and digital artifacts to design social justice curriculum in urban communities. *Northwest Journal of Teacher Education, 17(3)*, 22.

McCarthy, C., & Blake, S. (2017). Is This Going to Be on the Test? No Child Left Creative. *SRATE Journal, 26(2)*, 25-31.

Posner, D. (2004). What's Wrong with Teaching to the Test?. *Phi Delta Kappan, 85(10)*, 749-751.

Rezai-Rashti, G. M., & Segeren, A. (2023). The game of accountability: perspectives of urban school leaders on standardized testing in Ontario and British Columbia, Canada. *International Journal of Leadership in Education, 26(2)*, 260-277.

Suter, V. (N.D.) Folio thinking. https://vsuter.org/eportfolios/

Taylor, S., Agustin Paz, K., Rodriguez Zacarias, S., Griesan, M. & Heilman, J. "Blending Research and ePortfolio: Two HIPS in One." *AePR: The AAEEBL ePortfolio Review 7(1)*: (2023) 9-15.

WK Kellogg Foundation. (2016). *Truth, Racial Healing & Transformation Implementation Guidebook.* https://healourcommunities.org/wp-content/uploads/2018/02/TRHTImplementationGuide.pdf

20

Integrating PebblePad to adapt the Student-Led, Individually Created Course Model into a Master of Public Health Capstone Course: What we learned

Jennifer Yessis[1], Katherine Lithgow[2] & Nada El-Abbar[1]
[1]School of Public Health Sciences, University of Waterloo, CA
[2]Centre for Teaching Excellence, University of Waterloo, CA

The Context

This case study examines the adaptation and integration of the Student-Led Individually Created Course (SLICC) Reflective framework, developed by the University of Edinburgh, into a capstone course offered at the University of Waterloo. The capstone course is the required culminating course in the School of Public Health Science's Master of Public Health (MPH) program, which has been in place for 18 years and has been recently accredited by the Council on Education for Public Health (CEPH). The program is delivered online, with in-person requirements at the beginning and end of the program. It is possible to complete the program in 2 years as a full-time student, or 4 years as a part-time student. Students in the MPH program come with varying levels of expertise – some enter the program directly after completing their undergraduate degree with no public health experience, while others may have several years of experience in public health (e.g., nurses, data analysts, research associates, health inspectors, epidemiologists). To complete the program, students must develop 22 competencies related to skills needed for public health practice. The capstone course is designed to enable students to integrate these competencies into a public health deliverable for a client. Students are expected to attend one week of the course in person where they share their project with the class. The course size varies from 40 to 75+ students.

As the culminating experience in the University of Waterloo MPH program, the Capstone provides students with the opportunity to demonstrate two very important dimensions of their readiness to practice in public health:

- ability to collaborate with others whose backgrounds differ in important ways; these could include differences in discipline or profession, language, culture, values, ability and more; and
- ability to integrate lessons learned from a variety of sources and bring them to bear on a concrete public health problem. These lessons could include analytical tools or information from academic studies, practical skills gained from working during the practicum or from one's own job experience, and insights gained from personal experiences, civic involvement or reading.

Assessment of the first objective is based on the quality of the group products (oral presentation and written report), combined with peer assessment of each group's project overview and presentation describing their project. Each student is expected to provide feedback to other groups' project overviews and presentations. At this stage in the program, students have become experts in particular areas of public health practice; their peer reviews of group work will reflect the expertise they have. Assessment of the second objective is based on the completion of a PebblePad Workbook (each student completes their own Workbook) which includes a project proposal where the student describes the competencies that they will individually integrate for the project, reflections of peer reviews (on the project overview and presentation), and a final report that describes the student learning, reflections on the group experience, and lessons learned throughout as well as evidence of the individual contributions made to the group project.

Working in groups of 4-6, students are required to complete a project that addresses a particular public health issue. It can take the form of a program proposal, evaluation plan, policy brief, or an in-depth analysis of a public health problem.

Before the start of the course, students form their groups and meet with a public health client to identify a project and a useful public health deliverable that is of mutual interest to the students and the client. Throughout the term, the students work with their team members to complete the deliverable and present this to their peers and the client at the end of the term.

The Problem

Despite the project experience receiving positive feedback from students and public health project partners/clients over the years, the instructor was concerned that students "had the experience but missed the meaning" (Eliot, 1941). Students often did not recognize the transferable employability skills and other learning skills they were developing throughout the course. In addition, the instructor wanted to encourage more individual accountability while the students were working on the group project and allow each student to identify and articulate their own individual goals, and growth and development.

The Approach

The instructor had been introduced to the SLICC reflective framework while participating in a SLICC Learning Community offered through their institution and recognized the value that integrating critical elements of the SLICC model (e.g., student defined learning outcomes, reflection on feedback/process, an identified project of interest) might add to the capstone course. The SLICC model encourages students to identify the transferable skills they will need to develop, and ones they have and will deploy while completing a chosen project, and to develop the lifelong learning skill of intentionally planning for and articulating their growth and development, a skill that would serve the students well long after their graduation. The SLICC model promotes student learning by empowering students to adapt/personalize generic SLICC learning outcomes related to analysis, application, and self-evaluation to align with their interests and goals which results in deeper engagement in the learning process (Bovill et al. 2016; Healey et al., 2014). The model incorporates students' reflection on their experiences throughout their learning journey which has been reported to result in better articulation of their growth and development, and their ability to self-assess (Price et al., 2012).

Using the SLICC framework, students identified what they needed to do to achieve three prescribed learning outcomes, thereby taking ownership of their learning. In addition, each student completed reflections to examine their learning process.

Before the start of the course, student teams partnered with a public health client to identify a project and deliverable. At the beginning of the course, each student adapted and personalized three SLICC learning outcomes related to analysis, application, and evaluation, outlining how they would achieve the outcomes while completing the group project. Although the students were working on a group project, the personalized learning plan was unique to their individual needs (Speirs et al., 2017), thus making each individual accountable for their contribution to the group project. After personalizing the three prescribed SLICC learning outcomes, and to prepare for completing the client deliverable, the students met as a team to identify team learning outcomes, taking into account each individual's strengths.

The PebblePad platform facilitated the learning process in the following ways. Students used PebblePad to: 1) showcase their project with a group eportfolio, 2) complete individual reflections, and 3) provide and review peer feedback. As the capstone course size has been increasing from n=44 students in 2021 to n=75 students in 2022, PebblePad has helped facilitate scalability issues related to the integration of the SLICC model. Furthermore, incorporating the PebblePad reporting features made it easier to manage and compile peer feedback.

Students prepared a group eportfolio to present each project milestone, i.e., a project overview/group contract, a group project presentation, and a final written report with the client product. PebblePad feedback templates were used at each of these points to facilitate the peer and instructor review and feedback process.

Using a PebblePad template and Borton's model of reflection, "What? So What? Now What?", each student reflected individually on the peer and instructor feedback they received to determine what they needed to do or consider to enhance their learning. In addition, each student reflected on their unique learning process to consider what this meant for their future actions.

The Results

With funding from a LITE grant (https://bit.ly/LITE-grant), and with research ethics approval, we compared the reflections of students who completed the course using the adapted SLICC model with those from the previous course offering that did not integrate the SLICC model. Students who completed the SLICC model (via PebblePad) demonstrated:

- Deeper reflections with more specific evidence shared about learning.
- Greater recognition of transferable skills with specific examples provided (e.g., critical thinking skills, use of professional judgment when synthesizing the literature review, statistics, an environmental scan, and project management skills).
- Appreciating and valuing the expertise and perspective of peers via the peer review process.

- Ability to use feedback received throughout the project to improve the final product.
- Student growth and development as evidenced through reflections completed during the course. Students also expressed interest in continuing reflections in their careers.

Lessons Learnt

Learning curve

There is a steep learning curve for an instructor to effectively integrate PebblePad. Working closely with an educational developer with both technical and pedagogical expertise was necessary in this course.

Instructions and processes

It took time and thought to consider the processes necessary for students to use PebblePad in this course (e.g., creating a portfolio, completing peer review, compiling peer review from students, completing individual Workbooks for reflections). To make the process as seamless as possible, detailed instructions for students were needed each step of the way. To address different learning preferences, we created written instructions including screenshots, held open office hours to show students how to do each task, and created video instructions to visually walk students through the instructions in a recording.

Student perspectives about the value of reflecting on learning

Students in the MPH program are at different stages in their careers and lives; some students valued reflecting on their learning and the benefits that it provides, and others felt that the reflection component took time away from what they felt was the more important tasks of getting products completed.

Continuous evolution of Capstone Course over time

The course has evolved with continuous improvement after each course offering based on feedback from all stakeholders (students, Teaching Assistants, instructor) and from the confidence gained from applying the SLICC model. During the accreditation process for the MPH program, accreditation reviewers recognized that the integration of the SLICC framework supported the requirement of providing evidence of individual accountability within a group project.

Utilization of student reflections

Student reflections help an instructor understand how students develop through learning activities and provide information about what may and may not work in course delivery. Reflections also become a source of evidence of skills and detailed examples that instructors can share when asked by students to write reference letters for school, scholarships or employment opportunities.

In Brief

- Instructors must take a hands-on approach when integrating PebblePad into course design. They need to have a basic understanding of the workflow required for students to complete the learning activities using PebblePad, and for themselves, as instructors, to complete the assessment processes.
- A SLICC model can be used to demonstrate individual accountability for group projects. In this course, a PebblePad Workbook was used so that each student could identify learning goals and plans, share their work, and reflect on peer feedback and their learning experience.
- Leveraging class expertise through peer review is instructive to students and a valued part of their learning experience. Students reported that when different students provided the same feedback, it emphasized its importance. Students with strong expertise in particular areas provided their peers with valuable suggestions for improvement and helped them recognize their own expertise as well as the expertise of others.

Feedback

Student Quotes

Greater recognition of transferable skills:

> *"The project also helped me refine project management skills. We had a lot of work to do on short timelines. We were able to get it done by using excellent time management and delegation of work."*

> *"I developed critical thinking skills and using professional judgement when synthesizing the literature review, statistics and environmental scan, reviewing classmates feedback and developing recommendations for use in [project]."*

On the value of peer review:

> *"Students in the capstone course have provided meaningful feedback on the presentation and regarding our three main project components. Receiving feedback from my peers allowed me to become more comfortable with receiving criticism in terms of improving my approach. I think that this will benefit in the future in terms of collaboration within teams and stakeholders".*

On the benefit of reflections:

> *"This reflective process actually made me realize that one thing I would like to do is to pick 1-3 skills/core competencies to really focus on per year, and then seek out projects or work that aligns with these skills."*

References

Bovill, C., Cook-Sather, A., Felton, P., Millard, L., & Moore-Cherry, N. (2016). Addressing potential challenges in co-creating learning and teaching: overcoming resistance, navigating institutional norms and ensuring inclusivity in student-staff partnerships. *Higher Education,* 71, 195–208.

Eliot, T. S. 1. (1941). The Dry Salvages. In T.S. Eliot (Ed) *Four quartets.* New York, Harcourt, Brace and Co.

Healey, M., Flint, A., and Harrington, K. (2014). *Engagement through partnership: Students as partners in learning and teaching in higher education.* York, UK. Higher Education Academy.

Price, M., Rust, C., O'Donovan, B., Handley, K., and Bryant, R. (2012). *Assessment literacy: The foundation for improving student learning.* Oxford, UK. Oxford Centre for Staff and Learning Development.

Speirs, N. M., Riley, S. C., & McCabe, G. (2017). Student-Led, Individually-Created Courses: Using Structured Reflection within Experiential Learning to Enable Widening Participation Students' Transitions Through and Beyond Higher Education. *Journal of Perspectives in Applied Academic Practice, 5(2).* https://doi.org/10.14297/jpaap.v5i2.274

21

Empowering Community Care Licensing Education: Leveraging eportfolios for inclusivity, flexibility, and skill enhancement

Junsong Zhang[1], Albertine De Leon[1], & Ben Coulas[2]
[1]Centre for Teaching, Learning & Innovation, Justice Institute of British Columbia, CA
[2]School of Health, Community & Social Justice, Justice Institute of British Columbia, CA

The Context

Launched in 2013, the Advanced Specialty Certificate in Community Care Licensing (CCLO) is a 30-credit program designed to provide current and future community care facility licensing officers with the specialized knowledge, skills, and abilities that are needed to carry out the statutory duties delegated to them by the Medical Health Officer (Justice Institute of British Columbia, 2022).

Students pursuing this program are typically looking for a career as a community care facility licensing officer working for the British Columbia (BC) Ministry of Health. According to BC Ministry of Health (2016), community care facility licensing is one of the primary mechanisms used by the government to ensure that care and supervision provided to vulnerable persons meet minimum health and safety requirements. Community care facilities include child day care and residential care facilities for children, youth, and adults.

Students in the program typically come from a childcare background, holding diplomas in early childhood education, an adult care background with a degree in nursing or social work, or are already working as a community care facilities licensing officer. Many students in the program work as childcare providers in licensed home-based, private, and public daycare facilities. Most students take the program at the rate of one course per semester and finish the program in three to four years.

In the CCLO program, there are nine required courses including Administrative Law, Ethics, Inspections, and Investigations. All nine required courses are offered exclusively in an online, asynchronous format to accommodate learners working varied shift patterns in care facilities. In addition to the nine online asynchronous courses, to graduate, students must complete a final course of their choosing. The choice of the final course depends on a learner's background and preference. Up until 2021 there were two options for the final course:

1. CCLO-3409 - Learners already working in the field of community care facility licensing complete CCLO-3409 – Capstone Project in Licensing Practice. This is an online, asynchronous course where students are supported by their instructor to develop a research project related to an area of practice.

2. CCLO-3410 - Learners not currently employed as a licensing officer complete CCLO-3410 – Practice Experience. This course includes a six-week, full-time, practice education placement in a health authority.

While the program has provided these options to students, barriers still exist for students not currently employed in community care licensing who need to complete the practice education placement component. We will discuss more about these barriers in the next section.

The Problem

While the practice education course provided an excellent experiential learning opportunity, there were several issues with the mandatory six-week placement program structure that created barriers for student success and program completion and needed to be addressed. Some of the barriers related to completing the practice education course included:

- Having to travel to another part of the province due to the limited number of placements available in urban centres.
- For learners operating their own home-based childcare facilities, temporarily closing would leave parents without childcare.
- Being unable to provide the same level of support and flexibility for their dependents at home.
- Incurring additional expenses during the placement, including travel, meals, and accommodations.
- Having to close their care facility, take a leave of absence, or quit their job to attend the placement.
- Being without income for the six weeks.
- Due to lengthy waitlists for placements close to home, some students would need to spend additional time and money to audit additional courses in order to maintain their knowledge and eligibility for placement.
- Not having time to teach career search capabilities, including support in writing resumes and cover letters, as well as developing interview skills.

Additionally, the COVID-19 pandemic further reduced placement availability in health authorities and created travel restrictions, resulting in increased numbers of students on the placement waitlist.

Program administrators worked with health authorities to increase capacity for student placements with some success and, initially, a small grant was offered to support students financially while on placement. While these efforts did help some students, many students were still not able to complete the final course in the program. After learning about the required practice education placement, many prospective students already in the application process chose not to enroll in the program.

The barriers above caused significant problems related to reduced student satisfaction, graduation rates, and program admissions. The program area decided that action needed to be taken to address these barriers.

The Approach

Initial Design Considerations

Through consultation with students, stakeholders, instructors, program staff, and advisory committees, the design team decided that a third and new final course option should be developed to better accommodate the needs of prospective and current students. The new course, CCLO-3411 – Professional Practice, was developed in 2021 and piloted in early 2022.

The course is a 12-week online instructor-facilitated course, with synchronous and asynchronous components. The five main topic areas are covered in two-week modules. In each module, students complete readings, asynchronous activities, and participate in a synchronous, two-hour, evening or weekend session with the course facilitator and/or guest speaker(s). The synchronous session features various interactive activities, including topic discussions, role-playing exercises, guided case studies, and problem-based learning scenarios.

Originally, eportfolios were not included in the course design and assessment plan. However, the integration of eportfolios played a crucial role in enhancing the course design.

In discussions around the learners in this program, we identified the need for students to be better prepared to enter the job market and for future career development. Through review, we determined that students' job readiness could be demonstrated through project work that would document and showcase students' learning during and beyond the program. The use of eportfolios as a pedagogical practice lends itself well in the design process as it embraces authentic learning in the digital space and encourages the sharing of ideas, stories, and beliefs, resulting in enhanced knowledge production, application, and mobilization (Zuba Prokopetz, 2022). More importantly, an eportfolio is often considered as a tool for promoting, supporting, and enhancing employability, especially for those who are transitioning from university to the job market (Moretti, 2011).

With the pilot of eportfolios using PebblePad at the JIBC, the Centre for Teaching, Learning and Innovation (CTLI) provided a demonstration to the CCLO program staff, including both administrators and instructors, on the pedagogical practice of using eportfolio in different contexts and creating eportfolios and reflective learning through PebblePad, highlighting its potential, possible applications, and constraints. Upon careful consideration, we decided that integrating eportfolios into the course would be beneficial to students, faculty, and the program as a whole. Course assignments were then redesigned to include eportfolios as a way for students to curate and showcase the work they completed during the program while giving them the opportunity to develop their professional digital identity.

Course Code	
CCLO-3300 Administrative Law	All students
CCLO-3301 Vulnerable Populations in Licensed Care Facilities	All students
CCLO-3302 Ethics in Licensing Practice	All students
CCLO-3303 Lifespan Development	All students
CCLO-3304 Collaborative Conflict Resolution	All students
CCLO-3305 Human Relations	All students
CCLO-3306 Inspection, Compliance and Enforcement	All students
CCLO-3307 Investigations	All students
CCLO-3308 Professional Accountability in Licensing	All students

Course Code	
CCLO-3409 Capstone Project in Licensing Practice	Currently working in community care licensing
CCLO-3410 Practice Experience	Not yet working in community care licensing
CCLO-3411 Professional Practice in Community Care Licensing	Not yet working in community care licensing

Figure 1: The 2022 CCLO Program Structure, Featuring Three Pathways

Overall Design Framework

Given that our ultimate goal was to remove barriers, provide different pathways, and offer multiple means of actions and expressions, it made sense to consider the Universal Design for Learning (UDL) framework while designing the new course. The adoption of eportfolios perfectly aligns with these goals as it provides another option for reflective learning and supports students' professional development beyond the classroom (Takacs, et al., 2022).

Additionally, a working framework was developed to guide students' eportfolio development through our pilot programs. Drawing on the learning landscape framework (Tosh et al., 2006) and the conceptual framework for eportfolio (Mazlan et al., 2015), we find it beneficial to establish and incorporate the "Collect, Select, Feedback, Reflect and Share" elements in the processes to support students' skill development:

- First, students start with collecting relevant artifacts from their learning in the CCLO program, including reports, writing samples, and case studies; students were also supported in developing their professional resumes and cover letters.
- Then students select and determine which of their artifacts would be appropriate for their personal and professional development. In the collection and selection process, students are encouraged to focus on the integration and synthesis of

learning from various sources and formats, as we recognize that the learning is social and occurs inside and outside of the classroom. Therefore, it is critical for students to connect different sources of learning and map out their journey (Tosh et al., 2006).

- Throughout the duration of the course, instructors in the CCLO program review students' eportfolios and provide personalized formative feedback, helping to facilitate the mapping of students' learning journey. Additionally, instructors use rubrics that are specifically designed for eportfolio assignment to provide consistent and fair feedback for students.
- With formative feedback, students can further reflect on their personal growth over time. Through the feedback and reflection processes, students recognized their achievements, identified gaps in development, and acknowledged skills that require further work (Mazlan et al., 2015).
- Lastly, after the feedback and reflection process, students are encouraged to share their eportfolios with their peers, colleagues, and employers. By sharing their work with broader audiences, students may receive more feedback and suggestions and hence are motivated to further revise their work, resulting in an enhanced eportfolio and improved writing and communication skills. While sharing is encouraged, we have left the choice to the students, respecting that everyone may have a different preference on how they manage their digital presence and identity.

The "Collect, Select, Feedback, Reflect and Share" framework was instrumental in the design and development process as it captures the essence of eportfolio thinking and provided guidance on how we approached assessment, resources, and support for students and faculty. Given that the design framework described above is grounded in our pilot experience and largely inspired by the conceptual framework of eportfolios (Mazlan et al., 2015), it may or may not be applicable or suitable to other programs. It is our recommendation that leaders and practitioners in eportfolio development should analyze the specific needs and develop a process that works in their contexts.

Figure 2: The Conceptual Framework of ePortfolios by Mazlan et al. (2015)

Assessment Design

In the new course, CCLO-3411 – Professional Practice, we created six assignments ranging from evaluating applications, through inspecting a facility in the community, to building an eportfolio. In addition, students are expected to engage in discussions with their peers and the instructor in the online course and in the synchronous sessions. Overall, the assessment plan incorporates a variety of pedagogical methods with a strong focus on constructive, reflective, and experiential learning.

The eportfolio assignment is broken down into three smaller pieces so students have the time to orient themselves to the platform, PebblePad, and contemplate on their learning journey throughout the semester. A PebblePad orientation was provided by CTLI early in the course and students were provided with examples of previously created eportfolios. The course included this introduction:

"PebblePad is a portfolio and personal learning platform. It is designed to help learners, wherever they are learning (at study, work or play), develop, shape, and share their unique skills and attributes for success in today's world. PebblePad can be used by an individual to support their own learning and professional development, or by an organization to facilitate the learning of their members, be they students, staff, or professionals.

During your time in this program, you will have the unique opportunity of participating in our PebblePad pilot as we study the platform to see if it will benefit our students at the JIBC. For the next 12 weeks, you will utilize this online portfolio tool aimed to help you reflect on your learning as it occurs and to track your professional growth. You can collect, curate, and reflect upon your learning experience and demonstrate your knowledge. What you capture in this portfolio can be utilized for showcase or job hunting in the future if you decide to share it with the public or future employers."

Specifically, students are asked to complete three tasks that make up the foundation of their portfolio.

- The first task is to develop an "About Me" page to introduce themselves to potential visitors.
- The second task requests students to provide artifacts that exemplify their relevant work in the course or other pertinent areas, accentuating their knowledge, skills, and abilities. This encompasses their work experience, educational background, academic achievements, examples of coursework, and resumes.
- The third asks students to create a "Contact Me" page to share their contact information and links to other sites.

Even though there are only three required components in the eportfolio assignments, students were encouraged to collect and select their experiences from other sources of learning. As a result, some students went beyond the basics of the assignment requirements, producing more sophisticated and creative eportfolios that are both personally and professionally meaningful.

Implementation

Because CCLO-3411 was one of our initial pilot courses launched at JIBC, the initial setup lacked the complete integration between our learning management system (LMS), Blackboard, and the eportfolio platform, PebblePad, prompting modifications in the workflow to manually transition between the two.

To overcome this hurdle, we developed practical support materials for faculty, program areas, and students. Additionally, we conducted personalized synchronous training sessions and orientations. Throughout the semester, CTLI played a key role, providing continual support to faculty and students. We were readily available to assist with the eportfolio assignment and address any technical questions within PebblePad.

As our PebblePad implementation project progressed, we enhanced future iterations of CCLO-3411 to align with the improved communication between Blackboard and PebblePad. Subsequent deliveries featured a single point of entry for both platforms, seamless transitions from the course shell into the learner's eportfolio, and facilitated feedback and grading for instructors. We continually review, revise, and update our training and resources to align with the evolving PebblePad implementation, further streamlining course delivery.

The Results

The new course design has had a profound impact on students, instructors, and the CCLO program. The most significant outcome of introducing CCLO-3411 to students was offering a pathway to complete the program in a virtual online format. By implementing eportfolios into the course, students were able to map, reflect on their journey, and assemble their work with a focus on learning and career progression. It allowed for creativity and flexibility that provided a different learning experience. This was effective in a final program course where students had to consolidate their learning.

Students enjoyed more flexibility by having options to complete the program with a preferred pathway. The use of eportfolios fostered personalized learning and real-time feedback, enhancing skill development and job readiness.

By adopting and implementing eportfolio and reflective practice as a pedagogical strategy, instructors and program staff developed more capacity to support student-centred and life-long learning through the use of technology, which aligns with the BC's Post Secondary Digital Learning Strategy (Ministry of Post-Secondary Education and Future Skills, 2023). Overall, the integration of eportfolio expanded instructors' approach on reflective practices and fostered a more engaging environment for students to actively connect and evaluate learning from both formal and informal places.

As we continue to offer this course, less support is required for the instructor and students, but we are reminded that supporting students and instructors who are new to eportfolios or PebblePad is crucial in the success of educational technology adoption.

The change has also prompted a possible concern. After introducing the new, online, synchronous course using eportfolios, we have noticed fewer students opting for the CCLO-3410 Practice Experience course as their final course option. While this has reduced our waitlist for placements, we wonder if some students, who would have benefited more from the experiential and hands-on aspects of the full practice education course, are missing the opportunity in favor of the online final course. We continue to explore ways to reduce barriers while providing experiential learning opportunities.

Most significantly, the CCLO program is now able to support learners who would have been previously unable to complete a practice education placement. The use of eportfolios, serving as tangible evidence of student progress, provides insights for future program evaluation and refinement.

Lessons Learnt

Implementation and Integration

System integration plays a crucial role in students' learning experience. In our implementation process, the continued collaboration between Technology Services, CTLI, and the CCLO program staff and instructor made it possible to improve the integration, providing a better experience for students and instructors to develop eportfolios providing and receiving feedback, and reflect on learning beyond the classroom.

Support and Resources

Providing support and resources to students and instructors is at the heart of any design and implementation activity. CTLI provided ongoing and customized support for students in each new course, including presentations and demonstrations at the beginning of each semester, videos and step-by-step guides in Blackboard (LMS), and one-on-one sessions for students and instructors who need extra support.

Technology Barriers

As with any educational technology, like PebblePad or Blackboard, there is a learning curve which can increase the cognitive load of learners. It is important to be thoughtful in the design to avoid inadvertently creating another unnecessary barrier for learners. Inspired by Universal Design for Learning, we may consider offering eportfolios as one of multiple options for students to demonstrate their learning earlier in the program.

ePortfolio and Career Development

Broadly speaking, developing eportfolios for job search and career development in the field of public health is not usually a requirement. Even though there is some evidence that suggests using eportfolios could lead to an improvement in performance and self-regulation for healthcare professionals (Lai & Wu, 2016), it is difficult to gauge how much a student's eportfolio plays a role in securing a job or developing one's career. While we now have more tangible evidence of students' learning journey and skill development, the relationship between eportfolios and career development can be further investigated.

In Brief

- ePortfolios, aligned well with the principles of Universal Design for Learning, can enhance the accessibility of education opportunities and build different pathways for students. This is evident in the CCLO program as it now has three pathways for students to graduate.
- Building on different eportfolio frameworks, we found it beneficial to establish and incorporate the "Collection, Selection, Feedback, Reflection and Share" processes to support students' skill development.
- Implementing a new pedagogical practice such as eportfolio with technology like PebblePad may be challenging and overwhelming for students and instructors. Leaders and practitioners should carefully examine their needs and develop a support system that is responsive, and effective.
- Iteration is the key to the design! And the resources required for iteration are a result of our institutional commitment to innovation and educational excellence.

Feedback

Overall, the feedback we received from CCLO-3411 has been mixed with an increasing trend of positive feedback due to the improvements in the design of assessment, the integration of the systems, and skills and knowledge instructors and program staff gained over time.

From the instructor's perspective, the implementation of the eportfolio assignment is now more streamlined and easier to work with. However, in the initial pilots, user experience was an issue primarily due to the manual process that existed between PebblePad and Blackboard. This led to higher cognitive load and steeper learning curves. Students were also concerned about the replicability of their eportfolio work and whether it would still be accessible after graduation. This was due to the fact that PebblePad was newly introduced, and we had not formed an institutional strategy around how students may access their ePortfolios once they graduated from the program. As we continue with the implementation projects, we are more cognizant of this issue and the need to provide security and assurances to students and instructors.

Additionally, while some students suggest that certain features in PebblePad may not be user-friendly, such as uploading PDFs and PowerPoints, we have also heard excitement from students regarding how ePortfolios have supported the showcase of their achievements, professional aspirations, as well as their creativity.

Recent evaluations of CCLO-3411 reflect a growing positive learning experience from students. Nonetheless, we are aware that there are still areas for improvement, especially around support during the course and specific resources needed for eportfolio development.

References

BC Ministry of Health (2016). *A Guide to Community Care Facility Licensing in British Columbia.* https://www2.gov.bc.ca/assets/gov/health/accessing-health-care/finding-assisted-living-residential-care-facilities/residential-care-facilities/a_guide_to_community_care_facility_licensing_in_british_columbia_spring_2016_update.pdf

Ministry of Post-Secondary Education and Future Skills (2023, April 23). *B.C.'s Post-Secondary Digital Learning Strategy.* Digital Learning Strategy. https://www2.gov.bc.ca/assets/gov/education/post-secondary-education/institution-resources-administration/digital-learning-strategy/digital_learning_strategy.pdf

Justice Institute of British Columbia (2022, August 26). *Advanced Specialty Certificate in Community Care Licensing Program Handbook.* https://www.jibc.ca/sites/default/files/2022-09/Program-Handbook-for-Advanced-Specialty-Certificate-in-Community-Care-Licensing.pdf

Lai, C. Y., & Wu, C. C. (2016). Promoting nursing students' clinical learning through a mobile e-portfolio. *CIN: Computers, Informatics, Nursing, 34(11)*, 535-543.

Moretti, M. (2011). ePortfolio as a job-seeking tool for universities. *Journal for Perspectives of Economic, Political, and Social Integration, 17(1-2)*, 87.

Mazlan, K. S., Sui, L. K. M., & Jano, Z. (2015). Designing an ePortfolio conceptual framework to enhance written communication skills among undergraduate students. *Asian Social Science, 11(17)*, 35.

Takacs, S., Zhang, J., Lee, H., Truong, L., Smulders, D. (2022). *A Comprehensive Guide to Applying Universal Design for Learning.* BC Open Collections by BC Campus. https://pressbooks.bccampus.ca/jibcudl/

Tosh, D., Werdmuller, B., Chen, H. L., Light, T. P., & Haywood, J. (2006). The learning landscape: A conceptual framework for ePortfolios. *In Handbook of research on ePortfolios* (pp. 24-32). IGI Global.

Zuba Prokopetz, R. (2022). ePortfolio pedagogy: Stimulating a shift in mindset. *The Open/Technology in Education, Society, and Scholarship Association Journal, 2(1)*, 1–19. https://doi.org/10.18357/otessaj.2022.2.1.27

Index

A

accessibility	36, 57, 146, 151
accreditation	21, 50, 78, 106sq., 111, 115, 118, 134
achievements	43, 50, 54, 72, 77, 111, 141, 143, 146
alumni accounts	81-88
app	36, 111, 113
apprenticeship	123
assessment	6, 12-15, 26sq., 29sq., 32sq., 49, 51, 54sq., 61-64, 67-74, 76, 78, 80, 87, 89-93, 95, 97sq., 105-111, 113, 115sq., 118-120, 123, 125, 131sq., 135sq., 139, 141sq., 146
- practices	28, 107
- process	29-31, 62, 73, 78
- tool	14, 123
- workflows	30, 40
assets	32, 50, 67, 73, 75, 80-82, 87, 104, 111, 147
assignment	24, 30, 37, 40, 43, 45, 55, 69, 71, 101, 105, 111, 125-129, 139, 141-143, 146
ATLAS	30sq., 33-40, 50, 56sq., 73, 77-80, 91, 116, 123
attendance	11, 50, 115
Avery, Barry	66
Avondale University	5

B

Bachelor	26, 48sq., 61sq., 107, 115
Bassiri, Hailey	21
Bazela, Cat	26
Bell, Hailey	21
Blackboard	27, 30, 54, 143-146
blog	16, 44, 118
business	5, 16, 17, 35, 46sq., 66-68, 70

C

CASTL	14, 16
Cawthorne, Hadrian	26
Chapman, Brooke	115
Chmielewski, Robert	33
climate crisis	41-44
clinical	
- assessment	50
- experiences	76
- placements	48, 61
- skills	71sq.
cohort	14, 29, 49, 63, 68, 76, 103

collaboration	9, 41-43, 45, 54sq., 57, 62, 64, 68, 79, 101, 109, 114, 126, 135, 145
collections	50, 147
communication	8, 41-43, 46, 58, 66, 70, 74, 88, 109, 119, 126, 141, 144, 147
competencies	30, 41-44, 47, 49, 52, 123, 131sq., 136
- framework	54
Cooper, John	61
Coulas, Ben	137
counselling	5
COVID-19	49, 62, 64, 65, 78, 96, 138
CPD	123
critical thinking	44, 109, 114, 126, 133, 135
curriculum	22-24, 62-64, 66sq., 69, 71, 89, 92sq., 95, 103, 106sq., 111sq., 129sq., 142
cv	115

D

deep learning	125sq.
degree	61, 63, 68, 76, 87, 123, 131, 137
De Leon, Albertine	137
design	7-9, 12, 17, 21-25, 28, 35, 45, 49, 50, 52sq., 55, 57-59, 62-65, 73sq., 88, 91, 92, 93sq., 97, 107sq., 111, 112, 115sq., 119, 122, 126, 130, 135, 139, 141, 142, 144-147
dissertation	34, 105

E

Edith Cowan University	115
education	5, 8, 16sq., 24-26, 28sq., 32, 45-47, 53, 59, 61-65, 70, 76, 94, 106-108, 112, 125, 128, 130sq., 137sq., 144, 146sq.
educational psychology	26, 30
El-Abbar, Nada	131
email	11, 51, 62sq., 80, 87, 111
employability	66, 69sq., 116, 120, 132, 139
employer(s)	21, 22-24, 43, 66-68, 70, 123, 141, 143
employment	21, 53, 62, 64, 68, 115, 135
Engber, Dr. Kimberly	100
eportfolio(s)	5, 21-26, 24sq., 32, 34, 55sq., 65-66, 68, 70, 89sq., 100sq., 104, 122sq., 125sq., 129sq., 130, 133, 137, 139-147
- pedagogy	21, 24, 127, 147
evaluation	16, 24, 46, 62, 69, 74, 91, 107, 109sq., 132sq., 144

evidence	21, 30, 34, 36, 38, 43sq., 49sq., 55, 59, 62, 64sq., 67-69, 78-81, 86-88, 90, 109, 115, 118sq., 123, 126, 132-134, 142, 144sq.
experiential learning frameworks	33
external assessor	29, 31
extracurricular activities	68

F

feedback	13, 24sq., 27-31, 34-39, 43sq., 50-52, 58, 62-64, 70sq., 73-75, 77-80, 90, 93, 95-100, 102sq., 110sq., 115-120, 122, 127, 129, 132-135, 140-142, 144-146
- templates	35
framework(s)	28, 32, 41, 46, 54, 56, 65, 70, 89-93, 101, 107sq., 110, 115, 126, 131-134, 140-142, 146-147

G

Galleposo, Buena Jill	41
Gardiner-Klose, Sheridan	48
Gavilanez, Paola	21
graduate	22sq., 26, 66-70, 81, 87sq., 90sq., 106-109, 111, 117, 120, 137, 146
Grisedale, Dr. Louise	54

H

Harkness, Leigh	61
health	48, 50, 52, 54, 58sq., 61sq., 64sq., 71, 76, 106, 113, 131-133, 137sq., 145, 147
healthcare	54, 58, 61-64, 106, 109, 114, 145
higher education	1, 6-9, 17, 32, 46sq., 54sq., 60, 62, 66sq., 70, 89, 94, 106, 121, 136

I

identity	23sq., 47, 107, 110sq., 126, 140sq.
implementation	9-12, 14sq., 17, 23sq., 31, 41, 44-46, 51sq., 58, 71-74, 79, 89, 98, 101, 108, 115, 119, 123-125, 130, 143-146
- services	33
innovation	5sq., 9, 14sq., 46sq., 64, 98, 107, 109, 126, 137, 139, 146
integrated learning	61sq., 64sq.
integration	21sq., 27, 30, 35sq., 41, 57, 66, 69, 79, 106, 115, 117, 131, 133sq., 139sq., 143-147

interactive	56, 58sq., 139
interior design	21

J

Jaffray, Dr. Linda	61
job	11, 22-24, 66, 69sq., 87, 123, 131, 138sq., 143-145, 147
journal	14, 16sq., 25, 45-47, 60, 65, 70, 94, 102, 105, 112, 117, 126, 130, 136, 147
Justice Institute of British Columbia	137, 147

K

Kilgour, Peter	5
Kingston University	66
Kwantlen Polytechnic University	21

L

leadership	5, 7, 9, 15-17, 47, 61sq., 64, 76sq., 100, 102, 105, 130
learner identity	24
learning	5-11, 13-16, 21-28, 31sq., 34, 41-50, 54-67, 69-71, 73, 77sq., 81, 86-95, 99-112, 114-120, 122, 124-127, 129, 132-147
- and teaching	115
- experience	23, 46, 51, 54-59, 104, 135, 143-146
- management system	61, 67, 101
- outcome	109
- lifelong	54, 106sq., 109, 112, 132
Lees, Becky	66
Lindley, Jennifer	71
Lithgow, Katherine	131
LMS	50, 67, 69, 143, 145
Longhofer, Andrew	76
Lorenz, Susanne	41

M

Malone, Cathy	41
management	5-12, 14-17, 27, 35, 38sq., 47, 54, 57, 63, 70, 73sq., 76-79, 88, 109sq., 117, 133, 135, 143
marking	30sq., 34-39, 98sq., 110
Masters, Dr. Jennifer	81
McCabe, Dr. Gavin	89
McLaughlin, Paul	95
medicine	34, 54, 61, 71, 73

midwifery	48-54, 60, 65, 106
Midwifery Board of Australia	114
mobile	35sq., 75, 101, 108, 112, 147
Monash University	71
Moodle	50, 54, 79
motivation	10, 109, 111
multilevel	
- submissions	38
- workbooks	34sq.
multiple marking	33

N

National Health Service (NHS)	62, 65
nurse	59, 61-63, 65, 110
nursing	5, 48-51, 53, 54, 60-65, 71, 106sq., 109-114, 137, 147

P

Pacific University	76
participation	8, 52, 79, 136
patient care	76sq., 79, 107sq., 114
PebblePocket	34, 36sq., 51, 71-75, 108, 110, 113
pedagogy	5, 7, 9, 12, 14-17, 21-23, 56, 106-109, 111-113, 122, 124sq., 130
peer assessment	131
peer review	34, 58, 99, 132, 134sq.
performance expectancy	8
personal development	66sq.
personalised learning	115
Petrie, Kevin	5
pilot	6, 14, 62, 67, 69, 91, 100, 121-123, 139-141, 143
placement(s)	5, 26, 31, 48sq., 52, 61, 63, 65, 67sq., 115-119, 138, 144
portfolio(s)	11, 22-31, 33-34, 43, 45, 50, 55-56, 64-65, 67-69, 81, 84, 87, 90, 99, 108, 111, 113, 115-119, 121, 123-125, 129, 134, 142sq., 147
Portland State University	125
postgraduate	46, 48, 63, 91, 121
- programme	41
practicum	115, 131
presentation(s)	9, 24, 26, 87, 102, 131-133, 135, 145
Price, David	121

professional	10, 14, 16sq., 22, 25-28, 30sq., 33, 41-46, 54, 59, 61sq., 65, 67, 73, 76-78, 81, 84, 87sq., 91, 101, 106, 115-119, 123-125, 133, 135, 139sq., 142sq., 146
- identity	8, 41-44, 47, 61, 81

Q

quality assurance	30, 106

R

Redger-Marquardt, Dr. Chelsea	100
reflection	22sq., 31, 41-45, 50, 57sq., 61, 66, 68sq., 76sq., 89sq., 92-94, 98, 100-104, 108, 111, 115, 118sq., 123, 126sq., 129, 132-134, 141
reflective	11, 14, 22-25, 42-45, 47, 56, 68, 89-92, 95, 101, 103, 117sq., 128sq., 131sq., 136, 139sq., 142, 144
- blogging	33
- portfolios	33, 124
reporting	38, 40, 44, 63, 78sq., 118, 123, 133
research	3, 6, 9, 16sq., 21, 23sq., 57, 81, 87sq., 95, 101, 105, 112, 119, 126sq., 130sq., 133, 137, 147
Rihs, Jo-Anne	106
Riley, Prof. Simon C	89
Russell, Daniel	66

S

scaffolding	45, 56, 77, 103, 105, 110, 127
screencasts	30
Scriven, Rebecca	115
self-evaluation	108, 132, 142
self-reflection	23, 99
skills	14, 21-24, 26-30, 41-45, 47, 52-54, 58, 63, 66-71, 73, 89, 91-93, 106sq., 109, 115, 117sq., 131-138, 141, 143sq., 146sq.
- assessments	68
SLICC(s)	89-93, 131-135
social influence	8
software	51, 53, 95, 117
Spink, Joseph	121
STEM	46sq., 95
strategy	6sq., 26, 43, 51, 69, 88, 98, 112, 128, 144, 146sq.
structured reflective practices	23

student	8, 13, 22-24, 26-28, 30sq., 34, 36, 45sq., 49-51, 53, 55, 58, 61-66, 69-82, 85-92, 94-98, 100-105, 107-112, 115-119, 123sq., 126-129, 131-136, 138, 144sq.
- satisfaction	139
- success	21, 116, 125, 138
submissions	30, 33-38, 40, 69, 73, 78-80, 87, 99, 119
Sudlow, Gillian	21
summative assessment	30, 50, 68
support	5-11, 15-17, 21, 24, 30, 33, 37, 40, 44sq., 48sq., 51-53, 55, 58, 62-65, 67-69, 73sq., 76-81, 85, 88sq., 91, 93, 98, 100, 102-104, 111, 115-119, 121-124, 138, 140sq., 143-147
survey	62, 64, 66, 118, 127sq.

T

Taylor, Sonja	125
teaching excellence	21, 131
teaching	5sq., 8sq., 12sq., 15-17, 21, 25sq., 29, 46sq., 55-59, 61, 63, 89, 94, 98, 101, 105sq., 108, 116, 120, 122, 124-126, 129sq., 134, 136sq., 139
technology	5-9, 12-17, 25sq., 28sq., 45, 47, 55-57, 59sq., 62, 65, 70, 108, 112, 125, 144-147
- fatigue	5, 13sq.
template(s)	34-38, 37, 44sq., 50, 56, 63, 72-74, 77, 79sq., 113sq., 117, 126-129, 133
theology	5
The University of Edinburgh	89, 95
Thew, Harriet	41
training	5, 8, 10sq., 16, 26-29, 32, 44, 47, 49, 51sq., 59, 70, 72, 74, 76, 78, 122, 143sq.
transition	45, 52, 62, 81, 85, 111, 143
Turnitin	35sq., 39
tutoring	121-124

U

undergraduate	48, 62sq., 67, 70, 91, 95, 107, 110, 116, 121, 126, 131, 147
University of Birmingham	121
University of East Anglia	54
University of Edinburgh	33, 131
University of Leeds	41
University of Sheffield	26-28, 32
University of South Australia	48
University of Tasmania	5, 61
University of Waterloo	131

user	7, 13, 16sq., 35, 39sq., 51, 53, 55-57, 72, 83, 85, 104, 122, 146
- experience	33sq., 45, 72, 146

V

Valentine, Aaron	100
video(s)	26-27, 57, 63, 69, 87, 101sq., 103-104, 110sq., 113, 134, 145
virtual learning environments (VLE)	54sq., 57-59, 97, 122
vocational portfolios	33

W

web	87, 95sq.
Wichita State University	100
workbook(s)	28-31, 33-40, 49-51, 56sq., 57sq., 62sq., 67-69, 76-80, 90, 96, 99, 100, 102-105, 108-110, 113, 116sq., 117sq., 121-124, 126-129, 132, 134-135
workflow	10, 27, 30, 33-36, 50, 52, 63, 80, 135, 143
workplace	30, 52, 71, 112
workspace(s)	29, 34sq., 37-39, 50sq., 56-58, 63, 69, 76-80, 87, 123
Wylie, Bob	61

Y

Yang, Dr. Yang	61
Yessis, Jennifer	131

Z

Zhang, Junsong	137
Zoom	11

www.ingramcontent.com/pod-product-compliance
Lightning Source LLC
Chambersburg PA
CBHW071004160426
43193CB00012B/1911